Beyond
Quality

Beyond Quality

HOW 50 WINNING COMPANIES

USE CONTINUOUS IMPROVEMENT

JERRY BOWLES
AND

JOSHUA HAMMOND

G. P. PUTNAM'S SONS
New York

G. P. Putnam's Sons
Publishers Since 1838
200 Madison Avenue
New York, NY 10016

Library of Congress Cataloging-in-Publication Data

Bowles, Jerry.
    Beyond quality : How 50 winning companies use continuous
improvement/
  by Jerry Bowles and Joshua Hammond.
        p.   cm.

Includes bibliographical references and index.

    ISBN 0-399-13650-9
    1. Industrial management—United States.   2. Quality control—
United States.   I. Hammond, Joshua.   II. Title.
    HD70.U5B69   1991   91-16988   CIP
    658.5′62—dc20

Printed in the United States of America

1 2 3 4 5 6 7 8 9 10

Acknowledgments

One of the most remarkable characteristics of the American quality movement is the openness and willingness of companies to share information about strategies, practices, what works and what doesn't work, even with competitors.

In this book we present many ideas and thoughts gathered from literally hundreds of people we have met on our "quality journey." We listened to them, debated with them, and explored with them the limits of new ideas for improvement. We are indebted to each and every one of them for their time and insights.

In particular, we wish to acknowledge several special people who inspired, encouraged, and pushed us in our pursuits, innovations, and contributions to the movement. In chronological order these enablers are: John Hansel, president of ASQC in 1984–85, and Sandra Edson, former executive director of ASQC; both gave us room and support to try some new ideas for the promotion of quality nationwide that continue today.

Fran Hall of *Fortune,* who took a big risk on a special section on quality (introducing us to each other as writer and producer of these special sections) and cosponsored the first, and each successive, National Quality Forum. These *Fortune*-sponsored activities are arguably the largest and most far-reaching activities in quality improvement today.

Dana Cound of GenCorp, president of ASQC in 1986–87,

for his vision to establish the American Quality Foundation as an executive-led, research and development organization to look at the long-term issues of improvement.

The quality team whose invaluable editorial assistance supported the research and writing of this book are Brenda Niemand, Suzanne Bowles, and Chris Hammond.

And, finally, our thanks to Christine Sweeney of G. P. Putnam's Sons, for her invaluable help in turning our manuscript into a publishable book.

We dedicate this book to American business leaders whom we have met along the way and whose personal style of leadership we respect and admire.

To the executives who pioneered America's quality revolution: Jamie Houghton (Corning), John Hudiburg (Florida Power & Light), David Kearns (Xerox), Bob Galvin (Motorola), Don Petersen (Ford), John Young (Hewlett-Packard), and to the dean of quality executives—Roger Milliken.

To the new generation of quality leaders: Charlie Cawley of MBNA America, Ray Groves of Ernst & Young, Rosemarie Greco of CoreState First Pennsylvania Bank, Congressman Don Ritter (R–PA), Bob Stempel of General Motors, Frank Wells of Walt Disney.

Contents

Overview

GET BETTER or get beaten.

This powerful message galvanized the American business community in the 1980s as one by one the cornerstones of the U.S. industrial colossus—from consumer electronics to machine tools, automobiles to semiconductors—fell, or lost market share, to foreign competitors.

American industry, long the undisputed champion of the world, was suddenly revealed to be just another tired old heavyweight, easily battered by younger, nimbler competitors armed with speed and better fight plans.

The initial reaction to the foreign onslaught was a flurry of anti-free-trade activity. Tariffs, quotas, and "voluntary restraint" agreements were quickly put into place covering automobiles, textiles, semiconductors, and dozens of other basic industries. The total value of trade covered by protectionist measures nearly doubled during the first half of the 1980s.

Because of their enormous success in American markets, Japanese companies became the particular focus of intense, even shrill, cries of foul play. The apogee of the Japan hysteria movement may have come in a 1985 article in *The New York Times Magazine* by Theodore H. White, one of America's most respected journalists, who wrote:

> Today, 40 years after the end of World War II, the Japanese are on the move again in one of history's most brilliant commercial

11

offensives, as they go about dismantling American industry. Whether they are still only smart, or have finally learned to be wiser than we, will be tested in the next 10 years. Only then will we know who finally won the war 50 years before.[1]

Fortunately, many of America's best business leaders recognized that the real problem was a lot closer to home. The painful reality was that foreign competitors—mainly the Japanese, but also the Germans and East Asians—were winning the battle for the hearts and pocketbooks of American consumers not because of "cheap labor" or "unfair trade practices." They were winning because they were able to produce goods that had greater value than those produced by American companies.

Years of short-term management thinking, indifferent workers, outdated plants, low capital investment, and declining productivity had left America vulnerable to attack in virtually all of its basic industries.

The problem, simply put, was that the strategy for winning in the global marketplace had changed, but American companies had not. U.S. industry continued to focus on the mass-production paradigm in which the way to victory was to have smart people manage organizations that produced goods in large batches at low cost, leading to high profits.

Japanese competitors had developed a new and even more powerful paradigm: winning organizations are those that listen to the voice of the customer, design products and services that meet or exceed their expectations, and continuously improve *all* the organizational processes that lead to customer satisfaction. As a result, they were able to produce higher-quality products at lower cost and sell them at lower prices.

The real secret of Japanese success, perfected in virtual isolation over a forty-year period from the 1950s to the 1980s, is a customer-driven philosophy called *kaizen,* or continuous improvement, implemented through a formal process of company-wide quality control. In the West, these processes have come to be better known as "quality improvement" and "total quality management"—TQM, the ubiquitous acronym that covers a multitude of management practices.

We prefer the term "continuous improvement" because it

is less ambiguous than "quality" and more descriptive of the actual level of commitment required to make things happen. But in this book we often use the terms interchangeably because the distinctions between them are negligible to most people.

The major premise of continuous improvement is that by involving everyone within a company, from the boardroom to the mailroom, in a daily search for incremental improvements; providing everyone with the training, techniques, and authority they need to identify and fix problems; setting high-performance targets and measuring results; and focusing the company's strategic vision on the needs of its customers, everything a company does—every product, service, or organizational process—can be improved . . . forever.

Does it work? At the beginning of 1990, Toyota—the company that pioneered many of the techniques of continuous improvement and has been the world's most ardent practitioner of total quality management—was sitting on $22 billion in cash, enough to buy both General Motors and Ford at then current stock prices and still have $5 billion left over.

Beginning around 1980, a handful of the best American companies—Westinghouse, 3M, Hewlett-Packard, and a few others—began to recognize that quality was a major strategic and competitive issue. By 1984 the ranks of the converted had grown, and several dozen American companies had significant quality-improvement efforts under way, and were beginning to define the American version of total quality management.

Their efforts got a public relations boost in 1984 when the American Society for Quality Control (ASQC) persuaded Congress to create National Quality Month, an annual year-long educational and training program that culminates each October with special events and programs throughout the business, government, and educational communities. The campaign has been supported since 1985 by an annual special section of quality-improvement success stories in *Fortune* magazine.

The movement received another major shot in the arm in 1987 when Congress and then President Ronald Reagan created the Malcolm Baldrige National Quality Award—annual presidential citations given to companies that have made the greatest strides in improving quality and customer satisfaction with their products and services. Administered by ASQC, the Baldrige Award has quickly become the glittering prize of American industry and has helped rally business around a national standard of quality.

By the end of the decade, thousands of American manufacturing and service companies had adopted some type of total quality management. They had begun learning how to become more productive without building new plants or buying new equipment, how to turn waste into shippable products, how to cut inventory without sacrificing customer satisfaction, and how to enrich the working lives of their employees by making them part of the improvement process. They were learning that doing things better not only leads to higher customer satisfaction but also lowers costs and increases profitability. Many of their success stories are in this book.

A lot of progress has been made. The burst of restructuring and capital spending, labor productivity agreements, and reformed manufacturing processes that marked the latter half of the 1980s has left many of America's leading companies leaner and more competitive. That's the good news. But there is a downside.

Our fear is that the very popularity of TQM and the Baldrige Award could spell trouble because, frankly, quality—as defined by the current criteria for the award and the standards now being applied in American TQM—is not enough to keep U.S. companies on the leading edge in the years ahead. Rigorously applied, the Baldrige criteria are valuable guidelines that will produce results. But they are only part of the story.

One of the most discouraging conversations you can overhear in the corridors of corporations these days is speculation about how many years it will take for that company to become "Baldrige eligible." By that the speakers mean how long will it take to change the company's management policies, procedures, and practices; introduce and apply quality tools to functions other than production; effectively measure customer satisfaction; and engage the hearts, as well as the hands, of all employees, to a level that meets the requirements of the Baldrige criteria.

Most companies say they need three to five years. It is not

uncommon to see company documents targeting 1993, 1994, and so on as the year they will file for the award. "It's in the master plan—and by God, we're going to do it."

The danger here is threefold.

First, and most obvious, not every Boy Scout gets to be an Eagle. What happens to companies that spend three or four years getting ready to apply for the award and then lose? Will the CEO decide that "this quality crap doesn't work" and consign quality improvement to the executive closet, alongside "excellence," "management by objectives," and all the other quick-fix management toys of Christmases past? No matter that the companies' processes may have been improved enormously by the effort, some chief executives will focus only on the fact that they didn't win the award. Already some Fortune 500 companies we know have hired new vice presidents for quality specifically "to win the Baldrige"—after retiring their predecessors who failed to deliver.

Second, the Baldrige criteria do not address several elements of business success that we consider essential—*innovation, financial performance,* and *long-term planning*. Without attention to these issues, no company can be truly world-class. (We'll have more to say about this in Chapters 8 and 9.)

Finally, the world competitive environment will be significantly different by the time these companies, three or four years from now, have met today's standards. Many contenders may find that they've pressed the tux and bought the flowers, only to show up a couple of days late for the prom.

Don't misunderstand our point: the Malcolm Baldrige National Quality Award has proved to be a dramatic catalyst for improvement in American business. The number of requests for the application exceeded a quarter of a million in its first three years. And while the number of actual applications has averaged only seventy-seven per year, the number of companies that are using the criteria in one form or another for internal self-assessment is clearly in the thousands. Numerous companies have created chairman awards and company awards based on this internal self-assessment process.

But there is still plenty of work to be done—beyond implementing a quality improvement program or applying for the Baldrige Award—if American industry is to regain its dominance. Many companies have proclaimed their commitment to continuous improvement without fully understanding what it is or making the fundamental changes necessary to make it happen. Even in the best companies, progress has been uneven, with pockets of resistance still intact.

And, of course, foreign competitors have not been standing still. So confident are many Japanese companies of their ability to deliver quality and customer satisfaction that *atarimae hinshitsu* ("quality that is taken for granted") has become a common expression.

The companies that will prosper in the 1990s are those that have gone "beyond quality" to embrace the total requirements of competitiveness: leadership, concern for employees, innovation, environmental concern, reduction of waste in all its forms, and imaginative new ways to delight customers.

Our purpose in this book is to provide a perspective on how and why the quality revolution happened; define the key ingredients for making continuous improvement work; provide—through profiles—a look at the "best practices"—in our judgment—as they are now being applied by America's leading companies; define the areas beyond quality that need to be addressed; and suggest a framework for future development.

We've included the accomplishments of the winners of the Baldrige Quality Award, as well as a number of other pioneering companies. Some are obvious choices, like Milliken, Motorola, and Xerox. Some, like Emerson Electric and ServiceMaster, are not. Some are highly visible, like Corning and Hewlett-Packard; others, like MBNA America and US Healthcare, are not.

Our intent is not to single out these companies as being the "best"; they are simply those American companies that we think have made the most progress in improving the quality of their products and services over the past decade. They are also trendsetters, seemingly possessed of a sixth sense when it comes to planning for the future.

The book is divided into three parts. Part I addresses the past—the origins of the quality crisis in America; the value and limitations of quality control, the first tool for improvement; and an appraisal of two gurus (both Japanese) who in our opinion have had the greatest unsung influence on the quality revolution. Part II reports on the status of the quality revolution today, with profiles of companies that have made great strides by improving product or service quality or by focusing on the human side of quality. Part III looks to the challenges of the future—it profiles the companies that are now, and we expect will continue to be, positioned as leaders; it postulates our belief that in the long term quality is not enough; and it showcases companies that we see as the innovators, those with an instinct for quality and an insatiable desire for invention and renewal.

Most of the company profile material was developed during our research for the annual *Fortune* quality improvement section over the past six years. Other material came our way through Hammond's role as president of the American Quality Foundation and director of the National Quality Month campaign, as well as Bowles' research for his monthly newsletter, *The Quality Executive*. Over the years we've interviewed more than 100 CEOs, and in preparation for this book we've revisited a dozen or so—the leaders who helped define the quality revolution in America. We have visited most of the companies whose stories we are excited about sharing in this book.

Our message is simple: quality is a means, not an end. Without a solid foundation of continuous improvement, long-term profitability cannot be achieved, trust relationships with customers cannot be built, and the hearts of employees cannot be fully engaged. Continuous improvement in quality, customer satisfaction, *and* innovation is a strategic business issue of the first order. As we enter the second decade of quality improvement in the United States, it is clearer than ever that continuous improvement is a fundamental survival issue—companies that cannot consistently deliver improved quality products and services to their customers at competitive prices will not survive in today's global marketplace. The battle is far from over.

JERRY BOWLES
JOSHUA HAMMOND
New York, 1991

PART I

THE PAST

*What Went Wrong
and Why*

1 The 1980s— Decade of Crisis

In 1980 the average twelve-year-old kid with a paper route turned in a better financial performance than America's Big Three automakers. Chrysler was a ward of the government through a $1 billion loan-guarantee authorized by Congress. Ford lost $1.54 billion—the beginning of a three-year, $3.2-billion losing streak—and might well have joined Chrysler in the Washington breadline were it not for foreign sales, which accounted for 44 percent of revenues. General Motors, the largest corporation on the planet, posted a decline of $763 million—its first calendar-year loss in sixty years. Between 1950 and 1980, the U.S. share of the worldwide automotive market had plunged from 76 percent to less than 21 percent. And the automakers were not alone in their woes; the landscape was littered with fallen giants.

Suddenly it seemed that the United States, the mightiest industrial colossus in world history, was under attack on all fronts. Between 1978 and 1982, U.S. manufacturing productivity was essentially flat while the market value of the top 500 American companies declined more than 11 percent, not counting the effects of inflation. Although the United States had dominated the world in advanced manufacturing and technology for more than fifty years, 80 percent of American products found themselves challenged in the marketplace, compared to only 20 percent a decade earlier.

Foreign companies were rapidly closing the gap and—with a little help from their governments, whose notions of free market forces were radically different from those of the United States—had become the clear leaders in many important industries, from consumer electronics to computers and steel.

Among the first to fall was consumer electronics. In 1955, 96 percent of all radios sold in the U.S. were also made in the U.S. By 1965 the proportion was down to 30 percent, and by 1975 it was close to zero.

Although Ampex, an American company, held the original patents on home video recorders, it lacked the resources in engineering and manufacturing to bring costs down to the level of home systems, and Japanese firms quickly gobbled up that end of the market.

The $6 billion television market, which constitutes more than 20 percent of all consumer-electronics products sold, was also captured easily. By 1987 there was only one American survivor, Zenith, with a 15 percent market share. Two venerable American brands—RCA and GE—are now produced in Bloomington, Indiana, by the French company Thomson.

The warning signs had been there all along, but American business and government leaders had chosen to ignore them.

American companies pioneered the microelectronics industry, and all the major scientific advances that created the industry—the transistor, the semiconductor chip, computers—were American inventions. Yet America's share of the microelectronics market has declined rapidly. In semiconductor production, the U.S. portion of market fell from 60 percent to 40 percent during the 1980s.[1]

In March 1980 Richard W. Anderson, general manager of Hewlett-Packard's Data System Division, issued a chilling report that had a dramatic impact on the industry. Hewlett-Packard had inspected and tested 300,000 16K RAM chips from one Japanese and three U.S. manufacturers and discovered enormous disparities in quality. At incoming inspection, the Japanese chips had a failure rate of zero. The American-made chips had between 11 and 19 failures per 1,000. After

1,000 hours of use, the failure rate of the Japanese chips was between 1 and 2 per 1,000; the comparable rate for the American chips was 27 per 1,000.[2]

And on it went. The American steel industry, once the largest and most efficient in the world, suffered enormous declines in earnings and market share between 1975 and 1985. In 1964 the United States was a net exporter of machine tools; today it imports more than half.

How did it happen? The short answer is that American industry grew fat, lazy, and arrogant. It failed to invest in people, clung to outmoded methods of production, lost touch with its customers, and grossly—sometimes fatally—underestimated its foreign rivals. As a result, its products and services failed to meet the rising quality standards of international competition. Sooner or later individual companies faced their moment of truth. As Corning CEO Jamie Houghton says, "Nothing focuses your attention quite like the hangman's noose."

American business at the start of the 1980s was clearly in a quality crisis. Nonetheless, many American businesspeople simply failed, for a very long time, to make the connection between quality and such key measures of performance as cost, market share, and profitability. Quality ranked so low on the hierarchy of corporate priorities that a survey of institutional investors done in 1985 showed the quality of a company's products to rank last as a factor in influencing stock selection.[3]

A business community out of touch with customer expectations was clearly headed for trouble.

2 *Focusing on Quality Control*

THE UNITED States was the only major industrial country to emerge from World War II with its manufacturing capability intact. At the same time, there was a rising demand for consumer products to fill the void created over the years when production was directed toward the war effort. While other industrialized nations were recovering from the devastation of war and rebuilding their basic industries and infrastructure, the United States was pioneering entire new industries—plastics and fibers, semiconductors and computers, electronic instruments, jet aircraft, and industrial machinery. With little competition, American companies easily dominated the world in a seller's market.

To meet all this demand, U.S. companies expanded production capacity and invested heavily in new equipment. Scrap piles became first hills, then mountains, but managers reasoned that a certain amount of waste was the inevitable outgrowth of high-yield production. To recoup part of this cost, they poured money into repair processes. "Hidden" factories—entire production lines whose only function was to fix products that were defective the first time through—became standard operating units. Who cared if it cost twice as much to do something over as it did to do it right the first time? There wasn't any competition. At mass production, America was invincible. Or so it seemed at the time.

The American genius has always been the ability to produce serviceable products in great numbers at prices the masses can afford. Superior quality has been a secondary concern. Before the continuous improvement revolution, quality meant simply that products conformed to specifications; that is, a company's manufacturing operations produced—within certain tolerances—goods that met the specifications that design engineers gave them to work with. Often, these specifications—or blueprints—came in "over the transom" with little or no coordination between the two departments. Statistical methods were used to reduce variability during the manufacturing process and inspection-after-the-fact was supposed to weed out most of the defects.

To management, the notion of investing money in projects to further reduce the variability of a process that had a small defect rate, or was already producing within specifications, was an option rarely considered.

Quality control, not improvement, was the priority. At this point in history, one would tend to agree with the comedienne Lily Tomlin, who often wondered during her Broadway stage show of a few years back, "Why would anyone want to 'control' quality?" For the first half of this century, however, the system worked; it wasn't pretty, but good quality control was a competitive advantage.

The science of quality control, with its heavy statistical emphasis, is largely American made, much of it originally invented by divisions of AT&T. It was at their Bell Laboratories that Dr. Walter A. Shewhart first developed the science of statistical process control (SPC).

The current emphasis on an expanded approach to quality has tended to obscure the fact that quality control remains an important part of all manufacturing operations and a major weapon in the battle for continuous improvement. Statistical process control has made an enormous contribution to increased reliability of manufactured products around the world. Furthermore, you can't win the Baldrige award without it.

But the trouble with relying solely on traditional quality

control is its assumption that a certain number of products will always be defective and that finding them and weeding them out is more economical than fixing the process of making them. Because of this mind-set, which prevailed during the first two-thirds of this century, defective products became an unpleasant but common way of life in the age of planned obsolescence. So ingrained was the notion that perfection was impossible (or at least would cost too much) that suppliers were allowed to ship out parts at a one percent Acceptable Quality Level (AQL). That meant the purchaser had agreed to accept one percent defective parts.

The American Society for Quality Control (ASQC) produced a thought-provoking little booklet a few years back that dramatically illustrated the fallacy of thinking that 99-percent performance is acceptable. According to ASQC, it means:

- doctors would write 200,000 wrong prescriptions each year
- unsafe drinking water four days out of every year
- no electricity, water, or heat for about fifteen minutes each day
- no telephone service or television transmission for nearly fifteen minutes a day
- your newspaper wouldn't get delivered four times a year[1]

Except for a handful of quality professionals, who were pretty much the Rodney Dangerfields of corporate America anyway, few American executives in the 1960s and 1970s knew that the Japanese were playing the quality game by an entirely different set of rules.

There is a story told around Texas Instruments that is so good it must be apocryphal, but George Graham, TI's senior vice president and director of quality, swears that it is true. It seems that back in the late 1970s TI ordered a device from a Japanese supplier and asked that the order meet an AQL of one percent. Several days ahead of the delivery date, two boxes— one large, one small—arrived, along with a letter. The letter said, in essence, that TI would find 990 perfect devices in the large box and added, "Although we're not sure why you want them, you'll find 10 defective devices in the small box."

True or not, the story is revealing. During the 1950s and 1960s, while U.S. companies were basking in the triumph of mass-production and marketing genius over material costs, the Japanese were chipping away at the house that Ford built, honing their engineering and design skills, developing their work force, and reinventing manufacturing processes long considered the best way to "move the metal."

In a country with few natural resources, where frugality has long been a way of life, a manufacturing and service revolution was taking shape. The revolution focused on four primary goals—company-wide efforts to eliminate waste from every process, more productive and harmonious use of labor, zero defects in products and services, and an absolute commitment to meeting the needs of customers.

In short, the Japanese believed—and history has verified—that a management-led, customer-focused movement toward a goal of continuous improvement is a strategic business issue and a source of competitive advantage. By the time American management got the message in the 1980s, it was almost too late.

3 Lessons From the Japanese

WHAT ASTOUNDS many American managers even today is that most of the elements that constitute what the Japanese call "total quality control" (TQC) and Americans call "total quality management" (TQM)—systematic, company-wide continuous improvement efforts, self-directing work teams, employee-involvement programs, flexible manufacturing, quick changeover, customer focus, supplier integration, cycle time reduction—have been in place in some Japanese companies for more than forty years.

The Japanese like to credit pioneering American gurus such as W. Edwards Deming, Joseph M. Juran, and A. V. Feigenbaum with planting the seeds of quality improvement in their country during the late 1940s and early 1950s, and they certainly made valuable contributions. But for the most part this is a modern version of Tom Sawyer whitewashing the fence. Virtually all of the most important innovations in continuous improvement—*kaizen*—were made in Japan. They were developed out of that great mother called necessity.

While many individuals contributed to the Japanese miracle, two of the most important were Taiichi Ohno and Kaoru

Ishikawa. Their ideas basically shaped the "quality revolution," not only in Japan over the past four decades, but in America in the 1980s as well.

GIVING OHNO HIS DUE

There is an old Japanese saying that translates roughly as "the rice that is the richest with grain bows the lowest." Perhaps that's why Taiichi Ohno is so little known outside of the field of manufacturing. No one since Henry Ford has contributed more to the concept of modern industrial work. His ideas and techniques have not only transformed production processes in companies around the world, but they have also influenced the organization of work in service industries.

A modest, retiring man, Ohno was a brilliant self-taught engineer who developed the famed Toyota production system and created the concept of Just-in-Time, the most important single innovation in manufacturing (and quality improvement) since mass production. His engineering genius and production techniques are the basis of what is now called "flexible manufacturing" or "lean production," and he played a huge role in transforming Toyota from a small-car manufacturer near bankruptcy in the late 1940s into the world's third-largest automaker today, after GM and Ford. Oddly enough, Ohno's contribution to the quality improvement movement is often overlooked.

Born in Manchuria in 1912, the son of a Japanese ceramics technician working for the South Manchurian Railway, Ohno moved with his family back to Japan near the end of World War I. He graduated from Nagoya Technical High School in 1932 and began his career with Toyota's textile machinery operations that year. By 1943 he was an assembly shop manager in its vehicle-making operation. In the early 1950s he became Toyota's chief engineer. Over the next twenty-five years he built and continuously refined the most efficient production system in the world.

The basis of Ohno's thinking, which found its practical expression in the Toyota production system, is that all waste—

inventory, defects, time, excess plant capacity, unnecessary human effort—contributes to higher costs and lower quality. Thus, the goal is total elimination of waste.

Ohno's boss, Eiji Toyoda, a director of Toyota at the time and now president, spent three months at Ford's River Rouge plant in Detroit in 1950 and took copious notes, which he passed along to Ohno. They confirmed what Ohno had already suspected: the Ford system of mass production resulted in waste along every step of the production process.

The system was particularly wasteful in its use and deployment of people. The Ford approach assumed that workers would perform one or two simple tasks over and over. They were supervised by a foreman, who did no assembly work himself but ensured that line workers followed orders. Tool repairmen fixed tools. Inspectors checked quality and sent defective work to a rework area at the end of the line, where another group of workers made repairs. Because absenteeism was a daily and persistent problem, U.S. automakers also needed another category of worker called the utility man, to fill in where needed.[1]

To Ohno, all of this made no sense. None of the workers, beyond the line workers, were adding any value to the product. They were waste. Back in Toyota City, he began experimenting.

First, Ohno grouped workers together in teams, with a team leader rather than a foreman. The workers were given a set of assembly instructions and told to determine for themselves how best to accomplish the tasks at hand. The team leader performed assembly tasks in addition to coordinating the activities of the group. He also filled in for any absent worker.

Ohno next gave the team the job of housekeeping, minor tool repair, and quality-checking. Finally, once the teams were working smoothly, he set aside time for workers to meet with the industrial engineers, who still existed but in smaller numbers, to discuss ways to improve the process. Thus was born the modern idea of continuous quality improvement.

Ironically, it was these suggestion meetings—called quality circles—that nearly killed the American quality improvement movement in its crib in the late 1970s and early 1980s. Convinced that the whole Japanese secret was to get workers into a room and let them talk, hundreds of American companies launched quality circles with high expectations. The results were mostly disastrous. Meetings quickly turned into gripe sessions—about foremen, about management, about pay, about coffee breaks, about anything, it seemed, except how to improve quality.

As usual, American management had been cautioned by one of its own gurus but had not heard. A. V. Feigenbaum, writing in 1982, said:

> Western visitors to Japan invariably seek out the details of quality control circles and robotized operations to learn the basic keys to major Japanese improvements. Undoubtedly, these techniques provide benefits. But even the most enthusiastic proponent would recognize that quality circles have contributed probably 10 percent of the productivity and quality results in the typical Japanese plant . . . the productivity key is an attitude and the unrelenting application of that attitude within the framework of quality- and productivity-oriented management, much of it simply the hard-working, step-at-a-time variety very familiar also in American line management over the years. The visible techniques merely clothe the attitude and the management.[2]

In hindsight, the reason so many quality circles failed seems obvious. Once again, in its quest for the quick fix, American management had failed to look beyond the obvious.

One of Ohno's most inspired ideas was that the traditional mass-production practice of passing on errors rather than stopping the production line simply caused errors to multiply and become more expensive to fix. In 1961 he installed a cord (*andon*, literally "lantern") above every work station and instructed workers—all workers—to stop the line immediately if they spotted a problem. When this occurred, the entire team would come over to work on the problem.

More importantly, rather than simply regarding errors as random events, as was the practice in mass-production plants, Ohno trained workers to systematically trace errors back to their root causes through a problem-solving system he called the "Five Whys."

This system of error elimination works so well that Toyota's yields today approach 100 percent. That means the line is almost never stopped.

THE FIVE WHYS

In his system of the Five Whys, workers were trained to solve a problem by posing a series of questions which, when answered, would reveal the root cause. Masaaki Imai provides an illustration of how the technique works:

Question 1: Why did the machine stop?
  Answer 1: Because the fuse blew due to an overload.
Question 2: Why was there an overload?
  Answer 2: Because the bearing lubrication was inadequate.
Question 3: Why was the lubrication inadequate?
  Answer 3: Because the lubrication pump was not functioning right.
Question 4: Why wasn't the lubricating pump working right?
  Answer 4: Because the pump axle was worn out.
Question 5: Why was it worn out?
  Answer 5: Because sludge got in.[3]

The process traces the cause back to the real culprit and provides the real solution: in this case, attaching a strainer to the lubricating pump. By fixing problems at their source, workers made sure that they didn't happen again.

JUST-IN-TIME ARRIVES ON TIME

These innovations alone would have assured Ohno a place in manufacturing history, but he was soon to have another, even bigger idea, that was to influence quality improvement, inventory management, and supplier relations for decades to come. He meant to call this system in English "Just-on-Time," but it got changed in translation to "Just-in-Time." The name stuck.

The concept of Just-in-Time (JIT) is simple but powerful: materials and components should arrive at a factory, or from one work station to another within a plant, at precisely the moment they are needed for use. No sooner, no later. Parts are produced at each previous step in the supply chain just as they are needed at the next step. The mechanism for reordering is a simple token or card—with a description of the component and the number of parts needed—attached to the delivery container. As each container is used up, it is sent back to the previous step and becomes the automatic signal to make more parts.

Ohno called this "pull" system *kanban* ("shop sign") partly because he wanted Toyota to have a unique word for its system, but mainly because he wanted to confuse foreign rivals who might want to imitate it. This was in 1953, remember, when such a possibility was remote indeed. Nowadays, Just-in-Time and *kanban* are used by Westerners to mean the same thing.[4]

The consequences of shifting from the "supply push" method used in mass-production plants to this sort of "demand pull" arrangement are enormous. No costly inventory sits unused in warehouses, no bins of parts clutter the shop floor. Most important, from Ohno's viewpoint, even the smallest failure in the process causes the whole system to come to a halt. This has the effect of automatically improving quality because it removes all safety nets and focuses every member of the production team on anticipating problems before they happen.

Just-in-Time questions the very basis of mass production. The massive Western press lines were designed to turn out millions of a given part per year; Toyota was turning out only a few thousand cars a year at the time. Although the same press line could be used to make many different parts, the process of changeover presented major difficulties. For example, changing the 800-ton stamping presses used to turn out car panels often required a full day from the last part with the old dies to the first satisfactory part from the new die. Because the slightest misalignment could lead to disaster, the job was done by changeover specialists, while regular workers were idle.

All this meant that a press line had to turn out thousands of identical panels before it became economical to change dies. In some cases, presses were simply "dedicated" to turning out identical parts for months at a time.

Toyota had only a few presses at the time, and Ohno realized that either alternative—spending a lot of time changing dies or dedicating presses to specific parts—would not work at his company. More importantly, he realized that the tremendous batch sizes required by mass production made it impossible for manufacturers to respond rapidly to changing customer tastes and market conditions.

Ohno and his engineers set out to devise a better, faster way to deal with the problem of changing the dies that shape sheet metal in the giant presses. After much experimentation, they hit upon the idea of having all dies made to the same reference height so they do not have to be calibrated after being installed in a press. Instead of attaching the dies with nuts and bolts, the Toyota team used quick-release fasteners. This allowed workers—not specialists, but regular line workers—to slide a new die into one side of the press while the old one was being hoisted out of the way on the other side. As a result, the dies could be changed much more efficiently.

By 1970 Toyota had reduced the changeover time for a 1,000-ton stamping machine from more than a day to four hours. However, management wasn't happy because they knew Volkswagen could execute a similar changeover in two hours. Toyota sent for the brilliant industrial engineering consultant Shigeo Shingo who, over the course of six months, was able to get the time to an hour and a half. Another breakthrough brought changeover time down to three minutes and became another cornerstone of the Toyota production system.[5]

Two other features of the Toyota production system that are related to quality should be noted. Ohno realized that having workers attend machines that were functioning properly was a waste of time and energy. Therefore, all machines were designed to stop automatically whenever a defective workpiece is produced, shutting down the entire system until a thorough readjustment is made. This feature—which Ohno called *autonomation*—allows one worker to attend many machines, thus greatly increasing his productivity.

Finally, at the urging of Eiji Toyoda, who had picked up the idea at Ford, Toyota introduced its Creative Idea Suggestion System in 1951. Since then the company has received more than 20 million ideas from workers on how to improve the workplace. In 1988 alone, the company received 1,903,858 suggestions—representing participation by 95 percent of its work force—of which 96 percent were adopted.[6]

A key insight to emerge from Just-in-Time techniques is that moving to much smaller batch sizes improves quality. A machine operator who makes not 10,000 parts at a time, but 100 or even 10, is much more likely to spot a defect—say, a machine tool cutting out of line—immediately. If he doesn't, the next person in the production chain will. And he will do so in seconds, not days, and immediately trace the source of the problem. The possibility of thousands of defective parts piling up in inventory is virtually eliminated.

None of Ohno's Just-in-Time methods, you will note, have anything to do with robots or automation. Yet these decidedly low-tech methods have become the model for techniques used in mass-production plants around the world, including— among better-known Western examples—factories owned by Black & Decker, Corning, Motorola, Hewlett-Packard, Harley-Davidson, 3M, the Big Three automakers, and Johnson & Johnson. (It is amusing to read about how manufacturing executives at Johnson & Johnson "discovered" recently that they could eliminate trial-and-error adjustments on their packaging line by making a slide-in positioning fixture for each size carton that runs through the packaging machine. The fixture eliminates trial-and-error adjustments on ten movable parts that align cartons in the machine, reducing setup time to seconds and changeover costs by 90 percent.)

Edward J. Hay, senior vice president of the consulting firm Rath & Strong, summarizes the tangible benefits of JIT in the manufacturing companies that he has studied:

Twenty percent to 50 percent increases in direct and indirect labor productivity; 30 percent to 40 percent increases in equipment capacity; 80 percent to 90 percent reductions in manufacturing lead time; 40 percent to 50 percent reductions in the cost of failure (scrap, rework, and warranties); 8 percent to 15 percent reductions in the cost of purchased material; 50 percent to 90 percent reductions in inventories; 30 percent to 40 percent reductions in space requirements.[7]

But JIT is more than just a more efficient and quality-oriented method of managing inventory. A major residual outcome of Just-in-Time is that it revealed to the Japanese companies that first mastered it the value of time as a competitive weapon. Quite simply, they discovered that the JIT philosophy of waste elimination and time compression can be applied with equally significant results to all phases of the value-delivery chain—engineering, new-product development, customer service, logistics, and distribution.

For example, one of the best American illustrations of the JIT philosophy in action is not that of a manufacturer at all, but a service company. The distribution system developed by Federal Express to pick up and deliver packages to millions of customers every day is a marvel of synchronization and waste elimination. It was, and still is, FedEx's source of competitive advantage.

Amazingly enough, considering its obvious benefits, the Toyota production system—with JIT at its heart—was used in Japan exclusively by Toyota and its suppliers until the second world oil crisis in 1976. With their twenty-five-year pattern of continuous growth broken, other Japanese manufacturers realized that they were no more immune to peaks and valleys in manufacturing cycles than their Western counterparts. They began looking for ways to increase the flexibility of their manufacturing processes and discovered that the answer had been right there, in their backyard, for more than two decades.

W. EDWARDS DEMING: THE MAN AND THE MYTH

One of the great myths of the modern quality revolution is that it began with a series of eight lectures given in Japan in 1950 by W. Edwards Deming, recently dubbed "The Man Who Invented Quality" in an adoring biography. Born in 1900, the son of a rural Wyoming lawyer, Deming earned a Ph.D. in physics from Yale in 1927. He worked summers in Chicago at Western

Electric's Hawthorne Works, now famous for its pioneering studies of the impact of work conditions on productivity.

An admirer and colleague of Dr. Walter A. Shewhart, who developed the first statistical manufacturing control charts at Bell Labs in the late 1920s and published the classic *Economic Control of Quality of Manufactured Product* in 1931, Deming had first gone to Japan in 1947 to help the U.S. Occupation prepare for the 1951 Japanese census. While there, he met and socialized with a number of members of JUSE (Union of Japanese Scientists and Engineers), Japan's most important quality control organization, founded in 1946.

Deming biographers point in particular to a dinner at Tokyo's Industry Club on July 13, 1950, in which he told the presidents of twenty-one (in some interviews Deming says forty-five) leading manufacturers that if they would only use statistical analysis to build quality in their products, they could overcome their reputation for shoddy quality within five years.

One might reasonably wonder why so many senior business leaders turned up to hear an obscure Census Bureau statistician deliver a lecture on an esoteric, effectively untranslatable subject in a language that virtually none of them understood.

The answer is that both they, and Deming, had been invited by Ichiro Ishikawa, a wealthy industrialist who, in addition to being president of JUSE, had also served as the first president of Japan's Keidanren, the Federation of Economic Organizations. On the surface, FEO sounds like some sort of benign industry trade group. In fact, it is an organization with the power—sometimes exercised—to topple prime ministers and change the course of the nation.

Set up in August 1946 under the aegis of the government and the Occupation, FEO is an all-inclusive, all-powerful organization composed of more than 750 large corporations and 100 major national trade associations. It is the supreme coordinating body of what Americans call "Japan, Inc.," and its main purpose is "to maintain close contact with all sectors of the business community for the purpose of adjusting and harmonizing conflicting views and interests of the various businesses and industries represented in its huge membership. . . . It is the front office of the business community and is in effect a partner of the government."[8]

In 1950 refusing an invitation from Ishikawa was about as sensible as refusing a request from Don Corleone. It is unlikely, however, that Ishikawa wanted the business leaders there to be introduced to the concept of statistical quality control, for the simple reason that statistical methods had been introduced four years earlier and were already being widely promoted in Japanese industry.

A more likely reason for Ichiro Ishikawa's Deming dinner is that he wanted Japan's new industrial leaders to hear, from this tall, loud, terrifying *gaijin*—a slightly derogatory word used to connote anyone who isn't Japanese—what has been Deming's central message for the past sixty years: that they—management—were the problem, and that nothing would get better until they took personal responsibility for change.

And on that score Deming delivered. In a speech in Tokyo in November 1985, Deming recalled the dinner: "I did not just talk about quality. I explained to management their responsibilities. . . . Management of Japan went into action, knowing something about their responsibilities and learning more about their responsibilities."[9]

But, according to Kaoru Ishikawa, Ichiro's son, who would become Japan's leading quality guru, the Japanese quality movement made limited progress in the years immediately following Deming's 1950 visit. And, despite his father's pivotal role in bringing Deming to Japan in the first place, the younger Ishikawa maintained a deliberate distance from Deming throughout his life. In the Japanese edition of a book on Deming, Ishikawa noted that Deming had borrowed many of the ideas for his famous Fourteen Points (the first ten or so of which were written in the mid-1960s, not—as is often assumed—earlier) from Japanese TQC and J. M. Juran. It should be noted that this heretical passage does not appear in the English translation.

QUALITY CONTROL IN POSTWAR JAPAN

By the summer of 1950, when Deming made his dinner speech on statistical process control before Tokyo's Industry Club,

SPC was fast becoming a feature of Japanese industry. It had been introduced as part of the postwar reconstruction effort.

Shortly after Japan's surrender, the Civil Communications Section (CCS) was established by the Allied Command to help rebuild the country's telecommunications infrastructure. General MacArthur urgently wanted Japan to mass-produce radios so that Occupation authorities could reach every Japanese village quickly.[10] The section's small Industrial Division was assigned to work with Japanese manufacturers of communications equipment, whose products at the time were highly unreliable. Except for Homer Sarasohn, who had worked as a radio product development engineer at the old Crosley Corp. (now part of Textron), the group's key engineers—W. S. Magil, Frank Polkinghorn, Charles Protzman—had all worked at Western Electric or Bell Labs, the birthplace of American quality control. Indeed, it is Magil—not Deming—who is the father of statistical quality control in Japan, having advocated its use in lectures in 1945 and 1946 and successfully applied its techniques to vacuum tube production at Nippon Electric Company in 1946. (Ironically, NEC was launched in 1899 as a joint venture with Western Electric, which sold its stake in 1925.)[11]

From 1945 to 1949, the CCS engineers worked on a variety of projects, including establishing the Electrical Testing Laboratory to certify that quality standards were being met, advising Japanese business leaders on production management, and generally upgrading working environments. During 1949–50, Sarasohn and Protzman organized a series of eight-week courses on industrial management to which only top executives in the communications industry were invited. Among the students were Matsushita Electric's Masaharu Matsushita; Mitsubishi Electric's Takeo Kato; Fujitsu's Hanzou Omi; Sumitomo Electric's Bunzaemon Inoue; Akio Morita and Masaru Ibuka, the founders of what is now Sony Corp.[12] The courses were so popular that they continued for another twenty-four years after the Allied command was disbanded.

Kaoru Ishikawa was familiar with statistical methods through the Western Electric engineers' work at NEC and NTT and had been influential in helping JUSE launch a magazine called *Statistical Quality Control* several months before Deming's visit.

ISHIKAWA—THE GURUS' GURU

To a great extent, all of the American quality gurus labor in the shadow of Kaoru Ishikawa, who quickly recognized that the key to quality improvement was more than statistics, or motivation of workers, or turning quality into a management science—although all of these things are important. (Indeed, Ishikawa's *Guide to Quality Control,* written originally for Japanese workers, is now among the most widely read books in the United States on basic statistics for quality.)

Perhaps the most powerful contribution of Ishikawa and Japanese TQC to the worldwide revolution in continuous improvement is the recognition of two essential concepts: First, the whole point of quality control is "to develop, design, produce and service a quality product which is most economical, most useful, and always satisfactory to the consumer."[13] Thus, Ishikawa put the focus on the customer as early as 1950; most American executives began seeing the relationship between quality and customers only in the mid-1980s.

His second key concept was that quality touches every function within an organization and is everyone's job, not simply that of quality specialists. For Ishikawa, ". . . quality means quality of work, quality of service, quality of information, quality of process, quality of division, quality of people, including workers, engineers, managers and executives, quality of company, quality of objectives, etc."[14]

Ishikawa's definition neatly blends the major elements of Deming, Juran, and A. V. Feigenbaum and is widely accepted around the world today. The fundamental message is this: Commit to continuous improvement throughout the entire organization. Fix the problem; not the blame. Strip down the work process—whether it is the manufacture of a product or the performance of a service—to find and eliminate problems that prevent quality. Identify the customer, internal or external, and satisfy that customer's requirements in the work process or the final product. Eliminate all waste. Instill pride in performance, encourage teamwork, and create an atmosphere of innovation for continuous and permanent quality improvement.

The major reason these ideas were put into action so rapidly in Japan is a simple matter of Ishikawa's having been born in the right place at the right time. Unlike the leading American quality practitioners—Deming, Juran, Crosby, and Feigenbaum, who all came from modest circumstances and for many years had virtually no influence in business or government circles in their home country—Ishikawa was an aristocrat, born into the establishment of what was, and is, the most status- and class-conscious society on earth. He had the ear of Japan's most important leaders from the very beginning of his career.

Perhaps Ishikawa's most important contribution to the quality revolution was to provide the tools to "empower" workers. Having decided that everyone in the organization was responsible for quality, he realized that management had to provide workers with the training and methods they needed to measure the quality of the processes for which they were responsible. In 1956 he arranged to have the Japan Shortwave Broadcasting Corporation broadcast a quality control correspondence course for foremen. It proved so successful that NHK, the country's national broadcasting company, began offering a similar course on its educational television channel the following year. These courses were extremely successful in popularizing the concept of quality control.

Merging the ideas of Deming, Juran, Crosby, and Feigenbaum with his own and then distilling them into techniques simple enough for factory workers to teach to other factory workers, Ishikawa came up with the so-called Seven Tools now used widely in both Japanese and American companies. The tools are: Pareto charts, cause-and-effect diagrams, stratification, the check sheet, the histogram, the scatter diagram, and Shewhart control charts. Wrote Ishikawa:

From my past experience, as much as 95 percent of all problems within a company can be solved by means of these tools. These seven indispensable tools are sometimes likened to the seven tools of Benkei, the twelfth-century warrior. Unless a person is trained to use these simple and elementary tools, he cannot expect to master more difficult methods.[15]

With the exception of Joseph Juran, the American gurus have not been shy about promoting their role in helping launch the Japanese quality revolution. In this regard, Juran's modesty is most becoming. He has commented:

> A segment of the American press has come up with the conclusion that the Japanese miracle was not Japanese at all. Instead, it was due to two Americans, Deming and Juran, who lectured to the Japanese soon after World War II. Deming will have to speak for himself. As for Juran, I am agreeably flattered but I regard the conclusion as ludicrous. I did indeed lecture in Japan as reported, and I did bring something new to them—a structured approach to quality. I also did the same thing for a great many other countries, yet none of these attained the results achieved by the Japanese. So who performed the miracle?[16]

The simple fact is that the continuous improvement model being used in the best American companies today is Japanese company-wide quality control. The Japanese approach to total quality management—and its attendant successes—has had a far greater influence on the reemphasis on quality in the United States than the American gurus have had in Japan.

DEMING'S REAL CONTRIBUTION

Our slightly revisionist history is unlikely to make Deming loyalists happy, but his greatest contribution to the quality revolution may well stem from two spectacular, and seemingly accidental, public relations coups.

First, there are the prizes that bear his name. Knowing Japan's poverty, Deming refused any payment for his 1950 lectures and JUSE used the proceeds from reprints to create the Deming Application Prize, a prestigious award given annually since 1951 to companies with outstanding total quality programs, following a rigorous audit of their operations, and the

Deming Prize, an award given to outstanding individuals. The awards—medals bearing Deming's likeness—are given each year with great fanfare and attendant publicity.

Despite that measure of fame, Deming might well have remained relatively unknown in his own country had he not been "discovered" in 1980 by Claire Crawford-Mason, a veteran news reporter and TV producer, who was putting together a documentary on the decline of American competitiveness for NBC called "If Japan Can ... Why Can't We?"

At the suggestion of a faculty member at American University in Washington, she looked up Deming in his basement office in American University Park. She was amazed to find a man who seemed to know the answer to the program's provocative question living and working about five miles from the White House. Best of all, from the viewpoint of a TV producer in search of an exclusive, virtually nobody outside the rather arcane world of quality control had ever heard of him.

"If Japan Can . . . Why Can't We?" aired on June 24, 1980. The final fifteen minutes were devoted to Deming and his consulting work at Nashua Corporation, a New Hampshire manufacturer of carbonless paper.

Among other things, Deming told the interviewer: "I think people here expect miracles. American management thinks that they can just copy from Japan. But they don't know what to copy."[17]

The show was one of the most successful business documentaries ever, and it turned Deming into a celebrity literally overnight. The next day, his office was bombarded with phone calls. This was 1980, remember, and a lot of American companies were looking for something—anything—that might help them stem the tide of red ink.

Deming's message was a wakeup call for American industry. Across the nation, the best senior executives heard the alarm. Among the early callers were General Motors and Ford. In retrospect it is obvious that "If Japan Can . . . Why Can't We?" had only part of the answer, but it was clearly a major event in the quality improvement revolution that swept through thousands of American manufacturing and service companies in the 1980s.

PART II

THE PRESENT

What's Being Done

4 *Building the Foundation*

If, as Dr. Deming suggested on "If Japan Can . . . Why Can't We?" American managers didn't know what to copy, it didn't stop them from trying. Wave after wave of quality and manufacturing executives descended on Japan in the early 1980s, determined to unearth the "secret" of the Japanese miracle. Suddenly, anyone who had ever set foot in the Hotel Okura in Tokyo—or eaten sushi in San Francisco—became an instant "expert." From out of the woodwork, it seems, there appeared scores of self-proclaimed consultants, all eager to show companies the true way to quality. Each had his own map that promised secret byways, irresistible shortcuts, smoothly paved freeways. The American oracles—Deming, Juran, Crosby, and Feigenbaum—were suddenly in demand as never before.

The companies that devoted themselves to this quest for the quality grail concentrated their efforts, initially, on improving product quality. In many cases they simply copied Japanese TQC as closely as possible.

COPYING THE JAPANESE

For many American companies, the first glimpse of the Japanese approach to quality came from their Japanese subsidiaries. Hewlett-Packard, for example, found answers in a Japanese joint venture.

In 1978, not long after John A. Young became CEO of Hewlett-Packard, the world's largest and most diversified manufacturer of electronic measurement and testing equipment and second-largest maker of work stations, he ordered a comprehensive study of the venerable Silicon Valley company's operations to see what it would take to compete in the future. As part of that exercise, the company did an internal study of its manufacturing costs.

The results were instructive. Fully 25 percent of production costs were related to quality problems, to finding and fixing problems that occurred during the design, manufacturing, and procurement processes.

"At that time, manufacturing received less attention than research and development," Young says. "And manufacturing engineers didn't have as high a status or the pay level of those in R&D. Manufacturing people considered themselves to have a rather passive role, namely to build whatever R&D designed."

To better understand how other companies addressed the problem of quality costs in manufacturing, Young dispatched teams to the corners of the globe. Ironically, they found the answer they were looking for in Japan, at HP's own joint venture, Yogokawa-Hewlett-Packard (YHP).

Launched in 1963 mainly as a "window" into Japan, YHP had never been very profitable or quality-conscious. Then, in 1977, that changed. Over a two-year period, YHP cut manufacturing costs by 40 percent. By 1982 the failure rate of products had been reduced by two thirds, cycle time cut by a factor of three, and profitability had tripled. So dramatic was the improvement that YHP was awarded the Deming Prize that year. YHP won the Ishikawa Prize in 1988 and remains today one of HP's best-performing divisions.

What happened was that YHP management had seen the company-wide approach that other Japanese were taking to continuous improvement and had adopted total quality as a strategic goal. To get the effort off the ground, management picked a manufacturing process—printed circuit assembly using an automatic, wave-soldering machine that one of HP's U.S. divisions considered obsolete and had given to YHP in 1973. Before 1977 the defect rate on the machine was four failures per thousand. By the end of 1979—after two years of focus on total quality—the defect rate was down to 40 per million, and it has since fallen to three per million.

YHP's turnaround performance got John Young's attention in a hurry. In 1979 HP became one of the first American companies to adopt Total Quality Control as an operating philosophy. Young told his managers that over the next decade he expected to see a tenfold improvement—in scientific terms, "an order of magnitude"—in the reliability of HP's products.

"Why did I choose a tenfold improvement as a goal?" asks Young. "Because I wanted to force people to view their jobs in a different way. The magnitude of the challenge changed the way people in R&D and manufacturing viewed each other. It forced people to work across organizational boundaries. R&D engineers could no longer simply design products and then ask manufacturing to build them. They had to involve manufacturing people in the design at the beginning of the project. Because if the design wasn't easy to build, product quality would suffer. Teamwork has always been a value at HP. But TQC gave us a structured way to build on that tradition."[1]

The message that YHP's advances were the result of a change in the attitude of people, not an investment in new machines, was not lost on American managers. Rather than rush to automation, as so many U.S. companies were doing, HP put its emphasis on training its people and adopting productivity enhancements. The company was one of the first to adopt "Just-in-Time" techniques and to emphasize designing products that were simpler to make. HP remains one of the front-runners in the current "design for manufacturability" trend that has sharply improved manufacturing efficiency in factories throughout the world.

Bottom line? HP met its tenfold improvement target for the decade of the 1980s. The company saved $400 million dollars in warranty costs alone during the decade. Inventory levels dropped from 20.5 percent of revenue in 1979 to 15 percent in 1990—representing a savings of $541 million. Manufacturing productivity has risen dramatically, a 15 percent annual growth rate for the past five years.

MAKING QUALITY JOB ONE

If there is a classic example of betting the house on quality improvement, it is Ford Motor Company's development of the Taurus, the most successful new automobile launch of the 1980s. Conceived in 1980 and approved by Ford's top three officers—Philip Caldwell, then CEO; Donald Petersen, then president and later CEO; and Harold "Red" Poling, Ford's current CEO—at a meeting in Paris in 1981, the decision to go ahead with the $3.25 billion Taurus program was one of the most courageous in American business history.

At the time, Ford was bleeding profusely from the bottom line, posting a $3.3 billion loss during the 1980–82 period. And the most it had previously ever spent for the development of a new car was $800 million for the Fiesta.[2]

But Ford's management troika knew they had no choice. Unless they could produce a car that would dazzle customers, improve the company's reputation for quality (which surveys revealed was the worst in the industry), and streamline operations, the house that Henry built was destined for the dust bin of history.

The first thing the executives did was throw out Ford's traditional organizational structure and create a semi-autonomous group of developers called Team Taurus, headed by Lewis Veraldi. Veraldi segmented the team's mission into four basic parts:

- The team was to create a world-class car, with quality second to none—either domestic or foreign.
- The customer would be the focal point in defining quality.
- Product integrity would never be compromised.
- To accommodate the first three objectives, the team at

the very beginning had to involve people from both "upstream" and "downstream" in the carmaking process: that is, from the CEO's office to the design studios to the end of the assembly line—and even beyond, to the supplier, the ad agency, the dealership, and ultimately, the customer.[3]

It was a powerful vision and one that Ford's leaders knew would require radical new approaches. Rather than follow the traditional five-year sequential process for creating a new automobile, Team Taurus decided to take a "program management" approach. Representatives from all of the various units—planning, design, engineering, and manufacturing—worked from day one, with the entire team having responsibility for the final vehicle. That allowed problems to be resolved quickly.

The team also canned the usual "Detroit-knows-best" attitude and set out to identify the world's best-designed and -engineered automotive features so that as many as possible could be incorporated into the new car. Using a measurement standard they called "Best in Class," or BIC, Ford developers tore down, layer by layer, more than fifty comparable midsized cars and evaluated them in terms of 400 separate components. These 400 BIC items were grouped into twelve major categories and forty-nine subcategories, including ride, steering, handling, power-train smoothness, body chassis, performance feel, drivability, brakes, climate control, seat performance, and operational comfort.

"The object was to make the Taurus demonstrably better than competitive vehicles," says Veraldi. "We set out to try to match or exceed the competition in as many of the 400 categories as possible."

And Ford listened to its customers. By thoroughly surveying all its constituencies—customers, employees, suppliers, dealers—Team Taurus came up with a "want list" of 1,401 features that car buyers said they wanted. More than half found their way into the new models.

Besides the basic body design, which had the company worried since they weren't sure conservative drivers would accept the aerodynamic styling, the changes included coating the hood lever with vinyl to smooth its rough edges and color-coding parts of the engine to make it easier for car owners to do their own servicing. The one feature most often cited by customers as an unexpected added-value feature is a net basket in the trunk to keep grocery bags from tipping over.

Meanwhile, a five-member "ergonomics group" spent two years scientifically studying ways to make the cars comfortable and easy to operate. They took seats from twelve different cars, stuck them in a Crown Victoria, and conducted 100,000 miles of driving tests with drivers of all ages and both sexes, who were then quizzed on what they liked and didn't like. Dashboards and controls were also tested with potential customers to determine the quickest and most comfortable placement of instruments.

For the first time in Ford's history, the company actually solicited ideas from its assembly-line workers, even before the car was designed. The response was overwhelming, and many of the ideas were used. For example, workers complained they had trouble installing doors because the body panels were formed in too many different pieces—up to eight to a side. Designers reduced the number of panels to two. One employee suggested that all bolts have the same-size head so workers wouldn't have to wrestle with different wrenches. The change was made. (Astute readers will note that these are the kinds of things that Taiichi Ohno was doing at Toyota forty years earlier.)

The results of this "cultural revolution" were nothing short of spectacular. As consultants Alton E. Doody and Ron Bingaman put it in their book *Reinventing the Wheels*:

The first Taurus released in December 1985 met the target on 320 of the 400 selected BIC features—in other words, it matched or bettered a full 80 percent of the best features found on the best cars of its class in the world. By combining the BIC concept with other research, ergonomics, and true teamwork, Ford brought a "whole" product to market—whole in the sense of synergistically uniting in one car many of the best possible automotive features without having them cancel one another out.[4]

The results from the marketplace were just as enthusiastic. Largely on the strength of Taurus sales, Ford outearned General Motors in 1986 for the first time since 1924 and became the comeback story of the decade.

INVESTING IN QUALITY MODERNIZATION

For most of its sixty-six-year history, Caterpillar, the giant Peoria, Illinois-based manufacturer of earthmoving and construction equipment, had been king of the jungle. For many years the company had little competition. It built premium products, charged premium prices, and enjoyed fifty consecutive years of profits. Demand for Cat's trademark yellow products virtually always exceeded supply.

That all changed in 1982. The worldwide construction equipment market simply collapsed. High interest rates and a long recession brought construction to a virtual standstill in developed countries. The end of the energy boom and plummeting commodity prices meant that underdeveloped countries had no money to buy products or finance construction products. The dollar soared to new heights against most of the world's currencies. On top of all that, Caterpillar's unionized workers went on a seven-month strike, one of the longest walkouts ever endured by a major American company.

It was at this precise moment that the company's Japanese rival, Komatsu, pounced on the world market with high-quality products that were priced as much as 40 percent lower than Caterpillar was charging for equivalent models. The results were disastrous. From record profits of $579 million, the company began accumulating losses totaling $953 million over the next three years.

Faced with the Catch-22 choice of losing money or losing market share, Caterpillar management decided to sacrifice price to preserve market share. Although its North American market share dropped 11 points from 1981 to 1986 anyway, analysts believe the damage could have been much worse had the company not lowered prices.

"Obviously, we couldn't do that indefinitely," says Peter Donis, then president of the company. "It soon became evident that if we expected to remain a viable competitor in the global business environment, we had to make fundamental changes in the way we did business."[5]

Caterpillar management developed and set in motion a comprehensive business strategy whose cornerstones were continuous improvement, cost reduction, modernization, new-product development, and expansion into new markets.

Many of the changes were painful. Nine plants were closed and the work force was reduced from 90,000 to 60,000. Two-thirds of its factories were relocated outside the United States. Production was shifted from huge equipment like road graders and bulldozers to smaller equipment like tractor-mounted backhoes for home building and road repair. Between 1984 and 1989, Cat doubled its product line, going after markets it had never bothered with before.

The company made peace with its workers, establishing a profit-sharing plan for employees and a program called the Employee Satisfaction Process, designed to involve hourly workers in decision making and quality improvement. Thousands of its workers have been trained in quality improvement techniques such as statistical process control and design of experiments.

Caterpillar's most daring initiative was its Plant with a Future program, designed to modernize its aging production facilities. In 1985 it launched the PWAF plan to upgrade all 36 million square feet of its factory space—on top of the $850 million it planned to spend on machine replacement anyway. The company financed the modernization out of current revenue, which lowered earnings but allowed it to minimize price increases—a key factor in allowing it to beat back the threat from Komatsu.

By avoiding the Star Wars trap of technology for technology's sake and sticking to such "low-risk" devices as computerized machine tools, laser-read bar codes, and automated carrier systems—and by changing the layout of entire plants, not just selected areas—the PWAF program greatly speeded up assembly time, reduced inventories, and improved quality.

Caterpillar finished the decade where it had started—number one in crawler tractors and earthmoving and off-highway construction machinery.

CONNECTING WITH QUALITY

Few American companies have pursued the ideal of total quality with more determination or more success than AMP, Inc., the Harrisburg, Pennsylvania-based leader in the worldwide connector market. Since it launched its formal quality improvement process in 1983, the company estimates it has saved more than $60 million in quality costs.

AMP's dedication to quality has been reflected in the marketplace. Since it became a public company, the company—once described by *Fortune* as a "killer competitor"—has grown from $32 million in sales to about $3 billion, an annual compound growth rate of 15 percent, the corporate equivalent of gobbling up a fair-sized competitor whole. AMP commands 20 percent of a highly fragmented market contested by more than 500 competitors.

Virtually all U.S. employees—more than 10,000 people—have received training in methods improvement, error elimination, and statistical process control. Several thousand employees have received Value Adding Management (VAM) training and nearly 100 VAM project teams are now at work eliminating activities that add no value to the development, production, and delivery of products and services. AMP's highly regarded education and training program for engineers has delivered advanced instruction to about 3,000 participants in twenty-eight courses.

"Our emphasis on quality has earned us the reputation as the best-quality, lowest-price producer of critical components," says Harold A. McInnis, chairman and CEO. "But we're committed to reaching a tenfold improvement in fifty-four areas of customer service and product quality by 1991 and a single-digit parts-per-million defect rate by 1992. To do that, we must do more—we must engage the hearts and minds of every AMP employee."

The company's Plan for Excellence introduced in February

1990 is a major effort to integrate AMP's many successful quality, productivity, outsourcing, and related programs into a broader program built on a foundation of total employee involvement, greater commitment to employee training and development, and strong emphasis on leadership and cycle time reduction.

"The Plan for Excellence is structured around the guidelines of the Malcolm Baldrige National Quality Award because they happen to be the best quality guidelines around today," says James E. Marley, president and CEO. "We applied for the award in 1988 and learned a great deal, including the fact that while we were very good in a number of categories, we needed to do more to encourage a more participative environment."

The company's new spirit is particularly visible at its AMP Institute training facilities and at the new human resources building, completed early this year.

"If you really believe, as we do, that total employee involvement is fundamental to quality improvement, and that quality improvement is essential to total customer satisfaction, then you have got to find a way to get everybody involved," McInnis says. "The Plan for Excellence offers us a terrific process to do just that."

MANAGING INVENTORIES

Many workers at the Corning Inc.'s plant in Erwin, New York, remember all too well the winter of 1982 when a recession in the automobile industry forced a one-week closure of the factory, which makes ceramic parts for catalytic converters. The recession of 1990 could easily have produced a similar result. But despite losing 25 percent of its business during the year, about the same dip as in 1982, no shutdown was necessary.

The reason is that Corning, like dozens of other American companies, has adopted the Japanese-created Just-in-Time method for managing inventory, a process that allows the company to track swings in demand and avoid getting caught with stockpiles that can take months to use up. An excess of inventory was the major culprit in the 1982 closure in Erwin.

"Just-in-Time allows us to manage our inventory better in times of slack demand," says David B. Luther, Corning's corporate quality director. "The bonus is that it also tends to improve product quality, efficiency, and flexibility of work practices."

Before the Erwin plant adopted Just-in-Time in 1987, the factory followed what is facetiously called the "Just-in-Case" method. The company kept large supplies of everything it thought it needed. Inventory was warehoused at ten places inside the factory and in three leased warehouses. Total space devoted to storage was 185,000 square feet, the equivalent of six football fields.

Norman Garrity, who oversees manufacturing at Erwin and ten other Corning factories, sent senior managers out into the warehouses to find out just what they had on hand and to prepare a detailed map of how and when it would be used. The results were astonishing: only 6 percent of inventory at the plant was in use at any moment. Suddenly it was clear to managers and workers alike that excess inventory was waste.

Since the arrival of JIT, the Erwin plant now supplies its customers in days after the order is received, rather than the weeks it once took. Two of the three leased warehouses are gone, as are two-thirds of the stocks formerly piled up in the factory.

The savings are staggering. Carrying each $1 of inventory typically costs manufacturers 20 to 25 cents. Corning says the Erwin plant has so far saved more than $10 million and that its company-wide program to reduce inventory has saved about $180 million.

In addition to cost savings, the JIT program at Erwin has produced enormous dividends in both labor relations and customer service. Because it is better able to schedule production, Corning now gives one-month notice when it plans to scale back employment, and it plans to extend the warning to six weeks. Before JIT, workers could be laid off with one day's notice.

The company has also sought greater participation from its

work force. In 1989, it asked a sixteen-person team, including twelve hourly workers, to study quality and inventory procedures. As a result, the factory was able to further trim its inventories by eliminating several production bottlenecks. The plant now has one job classification for hourly workers, rather than the sixteen it formerly had.

The biggest payoff, however, has been in faster service and closer links with customers. Thanks to a new electronic-processing system, the Erwin plant now manufactures and delivers ceramic parts in less time than it took to simply confirm an order before JIT. Rather than specifying the week in which orders will be delivered, invoices now specify the day and even the minute.

If Corning is willing to learn from the Japanese, it is also willing to explore innovative new territory and invest in its people. Since 1984, when it began emphasizing employee training, return on equity has risen from 9.3 percent to 15.9 percent in 1989. Chairman James R. Houghton, one of the pioneers of the American quality movement, says, "In my gut I can tell you that a large part of our profit increase has come about because of our embarking on this course."

A good example: the company's new Blacksburg, Virginia, plant, which opened in 1989, operates on the concept of multi-skilled, team-based production, linked to automation. From more than 8,000 applicants, Corning picked the 150 with the best problem-solving ability and a willingness to work in teams. Although most of the new workers have finished at least one year of college, about 25 percent of their time worked in the first year was devoted to training in technical and interpersonal skills.

The investment was worth it. A team made up of workers with interchangeable skills can retool a production line to produce a different type of filter in ten minutes—six times faster than workers in traditional filter plants. This is a critical skill in a factory that constantly needs to switch product lines. Blacksburg turned a $2 million profit in its first eight months of production, instead of losing money in the start-up as projected.

In 1991 Corning planned to have its 20,000 workers spend 5 percent of their work time in classrooms, up from 4 percent in 1990, and far ahead of the 1 percent to 2 percent at most American companies.

Corning's experience suggests that combining Japanese manufacturing techniques with new American approaches to people and training can produce dramatic improvements in quality and productivity.

SUPPORTING QUALITY SUPPLIERS

JCPenney's commitment to quality is demonstrated by the fact that its Merchandise Testing Center was established in 1929. Today it is a 50,400-square-foot structure, housing a variety of engineers and technologists and equipped with the latest in testing technology and computer processing, which has enabled the center to double its testing capacity over the last couple of years.

Penney's maintains a global network of inspectors, over 100 in more than twenty locations throughout Central and North America. A corrective-action team of trained factory experts is available to assist suppliers worldwide and to conduct in-depth audits on produced merchandise. For suppliers these audits are critical, because Penney's rating on all aspects of a factory is a key variable in sourcing decisions and vendor appraisals.

The primary elements of the JCPenney Quality Assurance Programs include:

- Supplier testing requirements
- Federal requirements
- JCPenney care label policy
- Factory evaluation and merchandise inspection programs
- Corrective-action program
- Packaging requirements
- (Hassle-free) merchandise returns administration
- Product service program

One area in which JCPenney has demonstrated outstanding leadership is in its Minority Supplier Development Program, which was established as part of its affirmative action initiative in the early 1970s. The program was originally restricted to the merchandising department as a way to help expand the company's social and community-related programs. But it quickly outgrew that limited mandate.

In 1979 the program was expanded into a company-wide program. In 1990 the company purchased $328 million in goods and services from 1,973 minority vendors. In addition, the number of minority bank relationships maintained by the company increased from thirteen to forty over the past decade. In 1989 JCPenney maintained active accounts in twelve minority-owned banks and had lines of credit totaling $4.8 million in ten banks. The JCPenney Company Fund invested $3 million in CDs in thirty-one minority banks.

One of JCPenney's most innovative approaches to promoting minority business, both internally and to the outside world, is an annual national awards ceremony for suppliers and employees who have made outstanding contributions to developing the program.

"Minority business development is a two-way street, providing benefit to both minority business and to JCPenney," says chairman William R. Howell, who presents the awards. "These relationships work for the mutual benefit of both parties."

DEPLOYING QUALITY TO MEET CUSTOMER REQUIREMENTS

While many American companies are still struggling to master the basics of statistical process control and other long-established quality control methods, Texas Instruments, whose Japanese operations provided an early "window" into TQM, has begun to look to Japan for even more advanced techniques. One of the most promising of these is Quality Function Deployment (QFD), a system of new product development that helps engineers determine what customers really want and translates those requirements into engineering requirements. Developed by Dr. Yoji Akao, a professor of industrial engineering at Tamagawa University, around 1966, QFD was first systematized at Mitsubishi's Kobe shipyards in the mid-1970s.[6]

TI's Materials & Control group, headquartered in Attleboro, Massachusetts, as well as other groups around the world, have regularly been using QFD to solve a variety of problems. The system uses a chart that resembles a drawing of a house with a peaked tile roof and is often referred to as the "house of quality."

"My definition of QFD is that it is a system for bringing prevention to the design process," says Bob Porter, vice president—quality and reliability for the M&C group. "People have been talking for a long time about bringing prevention to the manufacturing process through SPC. In our business today, the real leverage is in doing it right at the design stage. Anything we can do when a product is still lines on paper has a hundred times more impact in terms of costs and customer satisfaction than trying to fix problems in the manufacturing stage."

QFD is a customer-driven system that attempts to get early coupling between the requirements of the customer, marketing, and design engineering. In a QFD chart, customer desires are grouped by category and written along the vertical axis of the array. The product characteristics are written across the top. The matrix is then used to check correlations.

"The idea is to let the product design be driven by the voice of the customer, not the voice of the engineer or, worse than that, the voice of management. After all, what do they really know?" Porter says.

The Materials & Control group has trained more than 400 employees in QFD techniques. One of its early applications was to an aerospace pressure sensor.

"This was very detailed; we learned a lot, developed some computer programs for doing the number crunching and so forth, but the bottom line was a real program killer," Porter says. "We discovered early on that the competition had a two-and-one-half-to-one advantage in one of the accuracy requirements. Without the QFD analysis, we probably would have built a device that didn't meet the customer requirements at all. By identifying the problem early on and addressing it, we were not only able to overcome it but to come up with a six-month cycle time reduction in the design and introduction of this new product."

The Factory of the Future

Imagine a factory where there is no work-in-progress, no finished goods inventory, and virtually no direct labor. Computer-integrated, its flexible manufacturing system can produce any number of units—including lot sizes of one—with absolutely consistent quality. For most manufacturers, the dream of such an automated "factory of the future" has been as elusive as it is seductive.

One of the few companies that have been able to pull off this plant floor miracle is Allen-Bradley, the Milwaukee-based subsidiary of Rockwell International. Orders for motor starters come in daily from computers in forty district sales offices and distributors. By the next day, each order has passed through twenty-six machines, untouched by human hands through assembly, testing, and packaging until reaching the shipping dock.

The computer-integrated manufacturing facility, which opened in April 1985, can produce up to 600 motor starters an hour in two sizes, but it also gives the company the flexibility to produce a special order, even a single item, without halting the line to change over machine tools. Manufacturing by orders alone eliminated the need for expensive inventories of parts to pile up. And automating the assembly line eliminates direct labor; only a handful of "attendants" oversee the operation.

The facility was one of the earliest American success stories in "simultaneous engineering"—designing the product and the production process together. A team of twenty-seven employees from marketing, development, quality, manufacturing, management information systems, and cost and finance were involved in the two-year design and construction process.

In addition to greatly reducing costs and improving quality, the facility also provides a bonus benefit: more than 60 percent of the equipment was built by Allen-Bradley and the plant serves as a living showcase for the company's factory automation products.

SUPPORTING DESERT STORM

When the final chapter is written on the 1991 war in Iraq it may turn out that the most important weapon in America's arsenal was not "smart bombs" but smart people. Embarrassed by the inefficiencies of a sprawling acquisition system that permitted such dubious purchases as $300 hammers and $600 toilet seats, the Department of Defense unleashed in 1988 a master plan to improve the overall quality of work and procurements made on behalf of the nation's defense establishment. That plan was total quality management (TQM).

No military command has more aggressively pursued the TQM concept than the Air Force Logistics Command (AFLC), a sprawling organization with 80,000 civilian employees and 10,000 military personnel, and capital assets of $158.3 billion (only slightly less than General Motors').

In 1988, then AFLC commander General Alfred G. Hansen, a Deming convert, broke with the traditional methods of quality control and instituted a quality program which combines four main components—people, process, performance, and product. The AFLC quality slogan is "QP4," defined as: Quality = People + Process + Performance + Product.

"TQM is participative in nature," says Colonel Darrell W. Grapes, assistant to the commander for quality, AFLC. "It empowers people to share their ideas for improvement and put them into action. The military, of course, is hierarchical in nature, so there is a widespread perception of conflict between TQM and the 'military way' of doing things. But, in truth, good military leaders seek information from their people and use it to make decisions. And they sure expect their people to participate in making those decisions work."

Since the QP4 initiative was launched, the AFLC has used its fundamental concepts for improving processes, reinforcing internal teamwork, recognizing outstanding team performance, and flattening the organizational structure by reducing layers of supervision.

Colonel Grapes believes the "new" AFLC culture played a major role in the superior logistical support and aircraft performance records in the Persian Gulf. For the people of AFLC, a huge payoff came on February 27, 1991, when General Norman Schwarzkopf said in a widely seen and quoted news briefing, "I can't recall anytime in the annals of military history when this number of forces have moved over this distance to put themselves in a position to be able to attack. But what's more important, and I think it's very, very important that I make this point, and that's the logistics bases. Not only did we move the troops out there, but we literally moved thousands and thousands of tons of fuel, of ammunition, of spare parts, of water, and of food out here in this area, because we wanted to have enough supplies on hand so if we launched this, if we got into a slugfest battle, which we very easily could have gotten into, we'd have enough supplies to last for sixty days. It was an absolutely gigantic accomplishment, and I can't give credit enough to the logisticians and the transporters who were able to pull this off."

5 Serving the Customer

"WHAT IS Quality? What the hell is it?" Readers of Robert M. Pirsig's quirky and brilliant bestseller, *Zen and the Art of Motorcycle Maintenance,* will recognize the voice of Pirsig's alter ego, Phaedrus, as he labors to come up with the perfect definition of the elusive word. To grossly oversimplify Pirsig's argument, Phaedrus decides in the end that quality is a combination of attributes that can be measured by "classical" scientific methods and the "romantic" baggage—perceptions, knowledge, experience, expectations—that each person brings to the object being considered.

Writes Pirsig: "If you want to build a factory, or fix a motorcycle, or set a nation right without getting stuck, then classical, structured dualistic subject-object knowledge, although necessary, isn't enough. You have to have some feeling for the quality of the work. You have to have a sense of what's good."[1]

Practitioners of traditional quality assurance methods underwent a similar journey of discovery in the mid-1980s as it became increasingly clear that improving the usual technical controls of the process of making a product, or delivering a service, did not necessarily cause those products or services to be preferred over others. Technical excellence was obviously important, but it wasn't everything. It was, and is, quite possible to make a perfect product or service that nobody will buy.

Out of this soul-searching came a key insight: quality is defined by customers' perceptions of value, not simply by adherence to strict process or performance specifications. As Peter Drucker puts it: "Quality in a product or service is not what the supplier puts in. It is what the customer gets out and is willing to pay for."[2]

By placing the emphasis on the needs and expectations of the customer rather than on simply improving the process, the new definition turned traditional quality thinking upside down. Slogans like "Do it right the first time," "conformance to requirements," and "zero defects" were quickly replaced by "the customer-driven company," "customer focus," and "listen to the voice of the customer."

In great measure, the movement from conformance-oriented to customer-driven measurements of improvement efforts was guided by the pioneering efforts of service companies like Metropolitan Life and American Express. These companies quickly discovered that the quality model being used by manufacturing firms had only limited usefulness in monitoring, evaluating, and assessing the quality of services. Similarly, a number of manufacturing firms found it difficult to apply the traditional quality control model to their service functions. Service quality was clearly different from manufacturing quality. The problem was that no one knew exactly what it was.

With the distinction between service and nonservice companies rapidly blurring, finding an answer was an important priority. Consider these astounding statistics: in 1990, 77.5 percent of GM's work force was white-collared and salaried, while only 22.5 percent were hourly blue-collar workers. At Mobil Oil, 61.5 percent of the staff was white collar; at General Electric, 60 percent; at Du Pont, 57.1 percent; at IBM, 91.5 percent.

Little wonder that Harvard Business School marketing guru Theodore Levitt declared: "There are no such things as service industries. There are only industries whose service components are greater or less than those of other industries. Everybody is in service."

About three-quarters of the American gross national product today derives not from producing products but from performing services. Similarly, about 75 percent of all jobs in the U.S.

are jobs in which success is measured not by how well products work but by how well customers perceive a service to have been performed.

Although it was clear that the concept of service quality had important implications for businesses in the service industry— as well as for the non-manufacturing operations of product makers—formal research was limited until 1983 when the Marketing Science Institute, located in Cambridge, Massachusetts, launched a major study of service quality by three professors from Texas A&M University—A. Parasuraman, Valarie A. Zeithaml (now at Duke University) and Leonard L. Berry.

Their findings—first published in 1984 under the aggressively unsexy title "A Conceptual Model of Service Quality and Its Implications for Future Research" and further refined in their 1990 book *Delivering Quality Service—Balancing Customer Perceptions and Expectations*—constitute the most important and widely used model of service quality yet developed.

Because so little was known about how quality was perceived by service consumers and providers, the professors began by conducting a series of consumer focus group interviews and executive interviews in four service sectors: retail banking, credit cards, security brokerage, and product repair and maintenance. Their objectives were to better understand what quality was from both the customer and provider perspectives, to find out more about what causes service problems, and to propose strategies for dealing with those causes.

Their first major discovery was the identification of four fundamental and universal characteristics that distinguish goods from services.

First, most services are intangible because they are *performances,* rather than objects. Because of this, they cannot be measured, tested, or verified in advance of sale to assure quality. When your car breaks down while you're on vacation and you call the local garage to come and fix it, you have no real way of knowing in advance how well the adventure is going to turn out.

Second, services—particularly those having a high labor content—are *heterogeneous.* The quality of the actual performance will often vary from provider to provider, from customer to customer, even from day to day. For example, American

Airlines is among the best-run airlines in the world, but we know very few frequent travelers who can't come up with a horror story of lost baggage, a flight that never got off the ground, or starting out for Jackson, Mississippi, and winding up in Jackson Hole, Wyoming. The damage from such disasters can often be minimized by intelligent handling by the company's employees. But even that is unpredictable. Not only does employee behavior vary from individual to individual, each individual employee may not consistently repeat the same behavior.

A third characteristic of service is that the *production is often inseparable from its consumption.* In the process of getting a haircut, for example, the service is provided and consumed simultaneously. Its success—or quality—depends upon how well the customer has communicated his specifications to the barber and how accurately the barber has interpreted and delivered what the customer wanted.

Finally, services are *perishable.* They cannot be inventoried, saved, and resold later. Flights that take off with empty seats or classrooms not filled to capacity have lost their value forever. This characteristic often makes it hard for companies to manage supply and demand.

Clearly, these four characteristics of service pose unique problems for organizations in terms of delivering what customers perceive to be high-quality service. As a basis for measurement, the researchers were able to identify the most significant factors that influence the customer's overall evaluation of service quality. These factors were grouped into five generic classifications: *reliability*—the ability to perform the promised service dependably and accurately; *responsiveness*—the willingness to help customers and provide prompt service; *assurance*—the knowledge and courtesy of employees and their ability to convey trust and confidence; *empathy*—the caring, individualized attention provided to customers; and *tangibles*—physical facilities, equipment, and appearance of personnel.

Using these five dimensions as a guide, the researchers designed a survey instrument called SERVQUAL that is able to quantify service performance levels by comparing the expectations of customers on the one hand and their perceived level of service delivery on the other. The "gap" between these two points represents the extent of a service problem.

With the gap model as a guide, one can identify a number of useful strategies that quality companies are using to meet, and exceed, customer expectations.

Listening to Your Customers

The movie *Big* provides an instructive insight into the value of listening to one's customers and knowing what they value. In the film, Tom Hanks plays a twelve-year-old boy who is transformed overnight into the body of an adult, while retaining his childlike appreciation for toys and play. Robert Loggia, as the CEO of a toy company, spots him in a toy store and recognizes him immediately for what he is: the perfect customer, more valuable than mountains of product research and lab tests. As a product tester, the Hanks character knows immediately what will appeal to kids, and his insight provides the company with a deadly competitive advantage.

American business prospered for many years with an "if we can make it, we can sell it" attitude. Product designers talked to marketers about as often as they talked to production engineers, which is to say, almost never. Meanwhile, Japanese companies were assiduously courting American consumers, uncovering and accommodating customer preferences. Toyota, for example, opened a design center in Southern California in 1973 to fine-tune its cars for American tastes.

Stung by the Japanese success, American companies in the 1980s began spending more time and money than ever before trying to find out just what customers want and incorporating those requirements into the design of their products and services.

Before Du Pont introduced its bestselling StainMaster fiber in 1986, a six-member team of marketing, R&D, and financial people spent three years surveying both retailers and the mill operators, who weave the fiber into carpeting, to find out how they thought StainMaster should be priced and marketed. As a result of these suggestions, Du Pont launched the fiber with the largest advertising campaign ever for a product. StainMaster became the most successful new product introduction in Du Pont history, bigger even than nylon, generating more than $2 billion in revenues in its first three years on the market.

By surveying its customers, Marriott discovered that a major complaint was the length of time it took to get breakfast from room service. In 1985 the company instituted a fifteen-minute guaranteed-delivery policy, and its breakfast business—the biggest share of its room service revenue—jumped 25 percent. The company accomplished this feat by getting employees to devise better ways to deliver meals on time, including having deliverers carry walkie-talkies so they can get instructions quicker.

Marriott guests find a postage-paid comment card in their room with "Will you let me know?" printed in large letters on the front. The company compiles the information in a Guest Satisfaction Index (GSI), which is part of Marriott's continuing commitment to finding out just what guests really want. In 1990 the company received more than 800,000 GSIs, each of which was reviewed by its Office of Consumer Affairs in Washington, passed on to management for review, and then sent to the individual hotels for action.

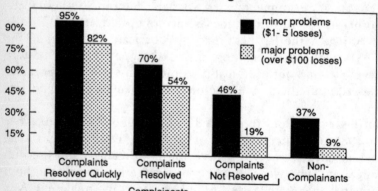

How Many Of Your Unhappy Customers Will Buy From You Again?

Source: TARP National Consumer Survey

BUILDING CONFIDENCE IN YOUR SERVICE

If American Express does a better job of pampering its customers than most service companies, it may be because it has been at it longer. During the 1970s, the company's Travel Related Services (TRS) business—best known for the American Express Card—was growing explosively, doubling the size of every facet of its business every three to four years. To maintain its standards and reputation, AmEx realized it needed a uniform, consistent quality assurance process.

"There were two major reasons," says MaryAnne Rasmussen, senior vice president, worldwide service quality. "First, we realized that if we delivered poor-quality service—which is the same thing as creating unhappy customers—it would cost us lost revenues and increased operating expenses. Moreover, it would negatively affect the future growth and profitability of our business. Second, we were convinced that since employees really wanted to do a first-rate job, if they were shown how to improve service, they would be happier, prouder, more satisfied, and more productive workers in the long run."

In 1978, long before any of its competitors got into the act, AmEx launched a new quality assurance methodology aimed at tracking, evaluating, and correcting the weak spots in its service delivery. Its goals were to define service from the customer's point of view; measure service delivery with the same objectivity that was used to measure productivity, costs and revenues; and, to involve all employees—line and staff at every level—in the quality service process.

Through market research and analysis of customer communications, the company determined that quality in the card business revolved around three characteristics: timeliness, accuracy, and responsiveness. Not only did people want on-time, error-free responses to their billing inquiries, but also knowledgeable, caring, and polite company representatives.

Once AmEx determined what customers wanted, it established exceptionally high performance standards and implemented a system to measure and monitor service on an ongoing basis. The system, now in place worldwide, statistically tracks performance for key transactions affecting the company's two groups of external card customers—cardmembers and service establishments.

The next stage was to get employees involved. "It's one thing to sell QA to management, quite another to sell it to employees," Rasmussen says. "As Casey Stengel put it, 'It's easy to get the players. Gettin' 'em to play together, that's the hard part.'"

The AmEx approach is a valuable model of how to go about winning the hearts of employees. First, the company involved employees from the start, bringing workers from different departments together to identify improvement possibilities through Service Improvement Teams. Second, it launched an intensive internal education and communication process that was both motivational and educational in nature—explaining why the standards were important. Each employee was told what was expected of him or her and how performance expectations, measured against established standards, would be an important part of each performance appraisal.

The company developed, and continues to use, more than 100 different recognition and reward programs, the pinnacle of which is the Great Performer Awards to honor individuals who have performed almost heroic feats on behalf of customers, e.g., improvising a travel office in the middle of a downtown street to serve travelers caught in Mexico City's earthquake.

Three years after the QA program was rolled out, the company's bottom line told a dramatic story. Not only had service delivery improved 78 percent, but expenses per transaction had been reduced 21 percent (and have since fallen even more). Within two years AmEx had reduced its cardmember application processing time by 37 percent. This single improvement added more than $70 million in increased revenues over the next decade and dramatically improved customer loyalty.

"With hundreds of millions of dollars added to the bottom line, there was no further need to sell QA within the company," Rasmussen says. "Everyone became eager to apply it to their line of business. So QA, which had begun with the card, expanded to traveler's cheques and other businesses."

Today, AmEx uses a complex process and methodology

called the Service Tracking Report (STR)—with more than 100 service measures—to monitor, track, and improve quality worldwide. Key service performance results, based on these statistics, along with action plans for improvement, are sent to and evaluated by New York headquarters, where a consolidated report of monthly performance is issued to all management around the world—including the chairman.

GOING THE EXTRA MILE FOR YOUR CUSTOMER

Most companies deal with two distinct kinds of services: routine services, which account for the bulk of their interactions with customers, and nonroutine services, which become necessary when a problem occurs. One of the key findings of the Marketing Science Institute research was that the way nonroutine service problems are handled is more likely to be remembered and passed on to others by customers than everyday occurrences. A company's reputation for quality service can be enhanced, or diminished, by the way it responds to problems or emergencies.

A dramatic example of this "value-added" service occurred a few years back when an electrical fire in Chase Manhattan Bank's main production site in New York City wiped out all of the fifty-story building's power—including all computer systems. This was the first day of the banking new year and Chase expected to process well over its daily average money transfer volume.

"Contingency planning is a continuous process for all applications—especially for critical ones such as money transfer," says John Fischer, New York area vice president of Digital Equipment Corporation. "When Chase purchased its equipment, we assisted in planning for the everyday and backup operations which are crucial to the bank's relationship with its customers. We also supported a secondary site, which was fully operational and configured to meet the backup processing requirements of the main production facility."

The situation for Chase was potentially disastrous. If on-line systems failed to process even one day's worth of transactions, the bank could be subject to serious penalties. The entire organization and its customers could suffer serious repercussions.

Two Digital field service crews were on the scene before dawn—one at the site of the fire and another at the bank's contingency site. Simultaneously, a Digital team from manufacturing, sales, and field service banded together, coordinating overnight delivery of additional parts and peripherals. That same day, the contingency site was fully operational, enabling Chase to successfully complete 95 percent of its business volume. Digital teams worked continuously with bank personnel until the main production site was back in business. For Chase customers, it was business as usual.

"Digital's response far exceeded any expectations I had, both in initially helping us get into a contingency mode and in ongoing support," says Jack Rosenstock, senior vice president at Chase Manhattan. "Much as our relationship with our customers gets built on a mutual sense of trust and support, Digital's support of us during that period has built a sound basis for an ongoing, strengthening relationship."

THE VALUE OF A QUALITY TRADITION

A company's values, traditions, and history are among the most powerful and often overlooked resources for instilling pride and the importance of superior customer service in employees. One company that has carried motivation by tradition to a high art is L.L. Bean, the legendary catalog and retail giant, headquartered in Freeport, Maine.

At Bean, workers at all levels receive classroom training—ranging from six days for order takers to two weeks for customer service representatives—designed to teach not only job-specific skills, but also the company's long tradition of customer service.

The first day of all training sessions—for its 2,600 regular employees and the 3,000 temporaries brought in each year to handle the Christmas rush—is devoted to the history and philosophy of L.L. Bean. A film chronicles the birth and growth of the company and is liberally sprinkled with homespun sayings from founder Leon Leonwood Bean. First among them is what Beanies call the Golden Rule: "Sell good merchandise at reasonable profit, treat your customers like human beings, and they'll always come back for more." The founder had a lot more to say about customer relationships, including:

> A customer is the most important person ever in this company—in person or by mail. . . . A customer is not dependent on us, we are dependent on him. . . . A customer is not an interruption of work, he is the purpose of it. . . . A customer is not someone to argue or match wits with. Nobody ever won an argument with a customer. . . . A customer is a person who brings us his wants. It is our job to handle them profitably to him and to ourselves.

Department heads come to the first classroom session to discuss the company's beliefs and its famous guarantee. The wording of the Bean guarantee is unequivocal: "All of our products are guaranteed to give 100 percent satisfaction in every way. Return anything purchased from us at any time that proves otherwise. We will replace it, refund your purchase price or credit your credit card, as you wish. We do not want you to have anything from L.L. Bean that is not completely satisfactory." If a customer returns a pair of boots after ten years, they are replaced, no questions asked. (Bean's return rate of 14 percent is well below the industry average.)

The company was founded in 1912 by Leon Leonwood Bean with $400 in borrowed funds and one product—a distinctly funny-looking rubber-bottomed, leather-topped boot that he designed himself. The Maine Hunting Boot, as it came to be called, performed the salutary function of keeping hunters' feet dry while they tramped around the woods, and it quickly caught on with local outdoorsmen. Bean's breakthrough inspiration was to get a list of people who bought nonresident hunting licenses (mostly Boston and New York professionals who liked to spend some time in the Maine woods) and send them a flyer advertising the boot—one of the pioneering efforts at direct marketing. Over the years, more merchandise was added, the mailing list expanded, the flyers became catalogs, and the rest, as they say, is history.

The company grew steadily, if unspectacularly, until its founder's death in 1967. By then, Bean had annual sales of about $4 million a year, 120 employees, and a coast-to-coast reputation among sportsmen for fair dealings with customers. It was also hopelessly saddled with outdated and inefficient systems. The average age of employees was sixty, files and letters were kept in cardboard shirt boxes, and workers typed over a million mailing labels a year by hand.

When Bean's grandson, Leon Gorman, took over the reins of the company in 1966, he immediately set out to bring the company into the modern age. He installed computers, commissioned market surveys to find out what customers wanted, and hired MBAs. Time-consuming processes such as opening mail and creating labels were automated. Customer service and toll-free 800 numbers were introduced.

Gorman's most important discovery was that the company had a far larger customer constituency than simply its original core of hunters and fishermen. The Bean name, and its honest, down-to-earth clothing products, struck a responsive chord with young and affluent urban dwellers—women as well as men. In 1979 Bean began printing catalogs in color for the first time, and during the 1980s ads began appearing in such seemingly unlikely publications as *The New Yorker* and *The New York Review of Books*. Thanks to L.L. Bean, by the end of the decade, thousands of people whose idea of the great outdoors is a cab ride through Central Park were roaming city streets looking as if they just came in from a hard day of fly casting on the South Fork of the Snake.

At the beginning of the 1990s, the company was filling about 12 million orders a year—an amazing 99.89 percent of them correctly. Bean's warehouse and distribution system has become the benchmark by which Xerox and other major corporations rate their own performance.

Robert C. Camp, who started the benchmarking program at Xerox, explains why:

> To the layperson, L.L. Bean's warehouse operation would not seem to resemble that of a manufacturer of packaged products. However, to the logistics professional, the analogy was striking . . . it was still a manual operation, carefully planned but

intensely directed by computer systems to minimize the labor content . . . the operation did not lend itself to automation because of the variety of sizes, shapes, and weight of items ordered by customers. The design relied on basic handling techniques to streamline the materials flow and minimize the picker travel distance. In addition, the design . . . was decided on with the full participation of the hourly work force, those who would have to operate the process.[3]

Today, L.L. Bean is an extremely sophisticated $600 million a year operation whose twenty-three annual catalogs—85 million mailings in all—offer some 6,000 items to consumers in the U.S. and Canada. The company's retail store in Freeport, Maine—complete with an indoor trout pond—has doubled in size to some 90,000 square feet.

The one thing that hasn't changed is the company's reputation for superior service. L.L. Bean is consistently rated the top mail-order provider in all the merchandise categories in which it competes. Leon Leonwood Bean would be proud.

PROVIDING CARING, INDIVIDUALIZED SERVICE

Elizabeth Mauras, a room service operator at the Crystal City Marriott, in suburban Washington, DC, received a call from a guest canceling a dinner order she had placed a few minutes earlier. Mauras noticed that the guest seemed distraught and asked if she was okay. She discovered that the guest had just received a call informing her that her mother in California had suffered a massive stroke and was not expected to live. The guest had called the airlines to book a reservation and was told there was only one flight leaving that night, and that was in thirty-five minutes. Assuming that she couldn't get to the airport in time, she had made a reservation for the next morning. As she was too upset to eat, she was canceling her room service order.

Mauras jumped into action. She called the restaurant hostess, briefly described the problem, and had the room service phones forwarded directly to the hostess. She then went to the guest's room, greeted her with a hug, and said, "Start packing.

I'll make sure you get on the plane tonight." As the guest packed, Mauras called the airline to change the flight, called the front desk to prepare the account, and contacted the bellstand to have a cab standing by and a bellman sent up to help with the guest's bags.

Because of Mauras' actions, the guest was able to arrive at her mother's bedside before she passed away that evening.

"In the competitive business world, we sometimes forget that caring people make quality service a reality," says Greg Behm, director, total quality management. "As for Elizabeth, her caring gestures and efficient actions ensured that we met the needs of one guest while continuing to serve all other room service guests that evening. While acts of empowerment are not always as unique as this case, they all involve finding a way to satisfy our guests." For her efforts, Mauras and her hotel were recognized at Marriott's 1990 Quality Forum.

Marriott has recently designed a video-based empowerment training program, using true-life situations to help associates learn how to be responsive to their guests while making prudent business decisions. Says Behm: "Learning how to remove the barriers and stay within the boundaries is the key to successful empowerment."

Says chairman and CEO Bill Marriott: "Businesses succeed, or fail, one customer at a time. If you treat customers right, they will keep coming back. We're working hard to ensure that all of our associates have been trained to make good business decisions and have been given the guidelines and authority to satisfy customer needs, whatever it takes."

Responding Quickly to Customers

Until a few years ago there was only one way for apparel manufacturers to get their products to market. The development of a new garment routinely required a lengthy and cumbersome series of sequential steps that consumed up to eighteen months from design to the scheduled shipment date.

Most apparel manufacturers still use this process. Once product designs are completed, samples are produced and presented to retail customers, orders are taken, and production levels established. Next, fabric is cut and sewn and finished garments—generally produced in large quantities to achieve economies of scale—are stored while shipment is arranged to the retailer's warehouse.

In 1987 Roger Milliken brought several apparel companies and retailers together to discuss a new idea called Quick Response, which allows manufacturers, suppliers, and retailers to be linked together through information technology. It was, most industry people agree, the most important meeting of the decade, with the outcome that many manufacturers now respond to an electronic purchase order in less than twenty-four hours.

To Lawrence R. Pugh, CEO of VF Corporation, maker of such famous names as Wrangler, Lee, Jantzen, and Vanity Fair, that simply isn't good enough for today's operating environment. Despite the enormous gains made by some apparel manufacturers through technology-based Quick Response programs, he believes the industry must do even more.

"The sad fact is that many retailers are out of stock on 30 percent of their items 100 percent of the time," Pugh says. "And this singular result creates disappointment and frustration to the consumer, headaches for the buyer, and chaos among suppliers of basic apparel products. It won't help to automate the system which produces this result. We must change the system."

To Pugh, true Quick Response can be achieved only when the process is arranged so that when a consumer buys an item, notice of the event is immediately available to all interested parties—the retailer, manufacturer, and the mill.

"If we can eliminate organizational barriers and encourage such a free flow of information, we can get a specific product replaced on the retail shelf in less than seven days—in an environment where sixty to ninety days used to be considered good practice."

In a major move toward meeting this challenge, VF Corporation has devised and implemented a Market Response System (MRS) designed to reduce cycle time and inventory, lower costs, and offer retailers and consumers the products they want, when they want them. MRS is executed through a series of simultaneous rather than sequential marketing, production, and supply activities, linked by information technology. When fully operational, the following actions take place at the point-of-sale when a consumer purchase is completed:

• The sale is recorded in the store, and stock information, such as style numbers, size, and color, is transmitted to both the retailer's headquarters and the appropriate VF division;

• Upon receipt of the data, the division automatically issues a purchase order, a warehouse picking ticket, and a shipping manifest for a replenishment garment, which will be sent to the store the next day;

• Point-of-sale data also triggers the manufacturing cycle to replenish stock within the division;

• Simultaneously, the retail buyer receives the point-of-sale information and, freed from reviewing store reports and purchase orders, concentrates on selling patterns and determines what, if any, stock adjustments are needed to respond to product trends;

• Based on the data, both the VF division and the retailer can identify slower-moving products for further analysis and tag popular items for replenishment or potential line extension;

• As garments are made to replace those sold, information is also shared with fabric suppliers and others involved in the manufacturing cycle.

To achieve its ambitious objectives, VF Corporation has set what it calls 40/30/20 targets—a 40 percent reduction in cycle time, 30 percent reduction in total inventory, and a 20 percent reduction in cost.

"By effectively implementing technology, sharing data, and building commitment among ourselves and all our employees, we can make it so that the consumer can count on having the right product, size, and color in the store every day," Pugh says. "In this way we build a foundation of consumer loyalty to us and to the retailer. And it is this loyalty that is necessary to sustain us through this decade and on into the twenty-first century."

Making Your Service Quality Visible

If you don't believe the Lord helps those who help themselves, you've probably never heard of The ServiceMaster Company of Downer's Grove, Illinois. Over the decade of the 1980s, the $2-billion-plus provider of services, primarily cleaning and housekeeping, to hospitals, schools, businesses, and large industrial plants, produced an average return on equity of about 65 percent—number one among America's service companies. In 1989 alone, the company's ROE was 150.4 percent.

ServiceMaster's stated objectives are "to honor God in all we do, to help people develop, to pursue excellence, and to grow profitably." Divine inspiration aside, the company's primary business is helping other businesses look good to their customers by providing the basic housekeeping, laundry, equipment maintenance, and food preparation services they can't, or don't want to, do themselves.

Ironically, it is precisely this often thankless work that is most visible to customers and contributes significantly to their impression of the quality of a provider's services. A hospital whose floors are chronically dirty is a hospital with a credibility problem with patients and visitors, who might be inclined to think that its medical services are of the same caliber.

ServiceMaster's senior executives know that motivating service workers is the key to improvement, and they expend an enormous amount of effort in imbuing what is generally considered grunt work with a sense of dignity and purpose. When the company takes over a site's maintenance activities, it brings with it a system of clearly defined career paths. It provides extensive training, even to functionally illiterate workers—one of its proudest commitments. (President C. William Pollard and his wife spend several hours each week teaching inner city Chicago kids how to read.) In addition, the company has assembled a vast reservoir of tricks of the trade developed at its headquarters laboratories, probably the world's largest lab for the development of industrial cleaning processes, materials, and products. The company's instruction manual for cleaning floors is three inches thick. Mop buckets are designed to hold only enough water to do a single room, ensuring that dirty water from one room won't be spread to another.

At heart, ServiceMaster never forgets that its role is to make intangible services, like cleaning, tangible in order to build credibility for its customers. On the eve of a new contract, senior managers descend on the facilities of a new account and lead the custodial staff through a thorough "break-in" cleanup of the premises. They pay particular attention to stripping and refinishing the floors of a hospital's lobby, which is, of course, the first thing seen by anyone entering on the first day of a new contract. Nothing energizes a maintenance staff or builds customer and employee loyalty better than the sight of a president or executive vice president expertly wielding a floor buffer.

Like the missionaries who went to Hawaii to do good, and did very, very well, ServiceMaster has discovered that there are profits to be made in doing humble work.

BANKING ON QUALITY

Skeptics say you can't measure quality in service industries like banking, insurance, and air travel. The skeptics are wrong. The Service Products Group of First Chicago Corporation, the nation's eleventh-largest bank holding company and the biggest banking organization in the Midwest, has been doing it successfully since 1981.

"We set out to increase the market share of our subsidiary—the First National Bank of Chicago—by positioning ourselves as the quality provider of corporate cash management services," says First Chicago president Richard L. Thomas. "These are noncredit services such as corporate checking, funds transfer, shareholder services, and so on. These kinds of services were traditionally considered to be 'giveaways,' designed to help build a relationship for deposits and lending. We believed they could become profit centers on their own, and that the best way to achieve that goal was to emphasize quality and view it as a strategic marketing weapon."

First Chicago's formal measurement program really began to take shape back in 1980. "We had a particular product quality problem—a system enhancement that was first delayed and then didn't operate as well as it should. We had to make sure the errors we had made in developing the new system didn't recur," Thomas recalls. "So we got all the key players into a room and we realized that we needed some form of measurement to judge how we were doing. There was a lot of disparity around the table about just what we should measure, however, and we finally concluded that there was only one valid opinion: the opinion of our customers."

The bank surveyed dozens of its corporate customers on a product-by-product basis, emphasizing two key questions about each of its nine noncredit products: (1) What do you consider quality features of each particular product? and (2) what do you consider good quality in the delivery of those features?

"We wanted to make sure we were doing the right things correctly," says Aleta Holub, vice president and manager, quality assurance. "We didn't want to be doing the wrong things right. By listening to our customers, we learned that what they most wanted and expected from us was timeliness, accuracy, and responsive service."

The next step was to ensure that the bank was satisfying those customer-defined requirements. An extensive performance measurement system using more than 500 charts was developed to track weekly every product area's performance in relation to a particular product or service. Using the customer's perspective and industry standards, managers from each unit established Minimum Acceptable Performance (MAP) standards for each indicator, as well as a goal for exceptional performance. At a weekly performance review, data on how each product area is doing relative to these demanding goals is presented to senior management. To encourage performance improvement, the MAP and goal lines are continually adjusted upward so that the carrot is always a little in front of the rabbit.

The commitment of managers to the program is considerably strengthened by the fact that a greater percentage of their bonuses is tied to attaining MAP and goal lines than to meeting budget. To avoid possible over-optimism, the bank's auditors spot-check the performance numbers tracked by the managers.

Does it work? Thomas says that since the program began, the bank has experienced significant improvement in each of its product lines. For example, he says that in 1982 the remittance banking lockbox operation was experiencing one error in every 4,000 transactions; today, that figure is about one error in every 10,000.

One of the most novel aspects of First Chicago's performance measurement program is the fact that customers and suppliers are regularly invited to attend and take part in the weekly meetings.

THE VALUE OF CUSTOMER SATISFACTION

Data/Facts:

- 10 percent of bank customers leave per year
- 21 percent of that 10 percent leave due to poor service
- Each bank customer = $121 per year gross profit
- Cost to acquire new customer = $150

Results (for a bank that has 200,000 customers):

20,000 leave × .21 (poor service) = 4,200
   customers

× $121 gross profit per customer	$508,200
+ cost of replacing lost customers (4,200 × $150)	$630,000
Annual Cost of Poor Service	$1,138,200

—May 1990 Report, American Banking Association

PARTNERING WITH CUSTOMERS

For most of the nation's 6,700 hospitals, logistics is an expensive and resource-consuming nightmare. For every dollar they spend on products like disposable gloves and gowns, sutures and therapeutic solutions, hospitals spend another dollar moving those products through their inventory management and warehousing systems. Baxter International, the largest manufacturer and distributor of medical supplies, recognized that solving the hospitals' problem could add value to its customer relationships—and contribute to Baxter's own bottom line.

Through an innovative distribution program called Value-Link, Baxter has become a full-time partner with many of its major hospital customers, taking over the managing, ordering, and delivery of its own medical supplies, as well as those of other manufacturers. Through daily Just-in-Time deliveries, Baxter fills orders in exact, often small, ready-to-use quantities and delivers directly to departments, including operating rooms and nursing floors.

This approach, called stockless delivery, is a major departure from the ways hospitals typically receive and handle supplies. Most hospitals receive medical products in bulk quantities delivered by numerous vendors. The large cases must then be broken down into small units and sent to the various hospital departments.

The Baxter approach can reduce or eliminate the need for hospitals to warehouse products. St. Luke's Episcopal Hospital in Houston, for example, estimates that it has saved $1.5 million a year since it adopted the Baxter system in 1988.

"When you deal with customers in such a critical area on a daily basis, you have to have a lot of confidence in your ability to deliver," says Ronald H. Abrahams, Baxter's vice president, quality assurance and regulatory affairs. "Our Quality Leadership Process (QLP) plays a key role in allowing us to meet the demanding requirements of our customers."

CENTRALIZING CUSTOMER SERVICE

Management at Fidelity Bank of Philadelphia hired Technical Assistance Research Programs (TARP), a Washington, D.C.-based consulting firm, to take a look at its decentralized service system in late 1986 and was dismayed at the results. Only 58 percent of Fidelity's customers were satisfied with existing service levels. The only good news was that customers regarded all the other banks in the area as equally bad.

For Fidelity president Rosemarie B. Greco (now CEO of CoreState First Pennsylvania Bank), that wasn't consolation enough. She put together a service improvement task force, consisting of ten individuals representing operations, systems, the branches, community commercial banking, and corporate planning, to develop a strategy to make service a competitive advantage for Fidelity.

Following extensive surveys of customers and Fidelity's own personnel, the team identified a number of problems. Among them:

• Many noncontact staff received phone calls from customers, which they tried to handle (often inefficiently).

• Contact personnel were measured and rewarded on sales related to productivity, not quality.

• Employees lacked the authority, training, and confidence to solve problems on their own.

• There was no system to log or track customer contacts. This limited the accountability for solving a problem or performing an analysis of customer contact data in order to prevent their recurrence.

• A significant number of calls were misdirected throughout the organization.

The basic strategy developed out of these findings was to create a single, high-quality service unit that would be easy for customers to contact, upgrade the status and training of service personnel, and revamp support systems. The bank invested $3 million to launch its Centralized Customer Service Center in 1987. Fidelity management says the center has not only allowed the bank to meet its goal of differentiating Fidelity through superior service, it has saved more than $1 million a year in operating costs. Among the other positive results:

• The center now handles more than 175,000 contacts a month, versus 30,000 under the old decentralized system.

• Service units costs have decreased 22 percent and opportunities for cross-selling have increased 57 percent.

• Customer satisfaction has risen from 58 percent to more than 90 percent.

"We've demonstrated that quality service can have a major positive impact on a bank's revenue and market share as well as on its ability to sell additional products to existing customers," Greco says. "But merely saying that service quality is important is not enough. You have to take direct actions that increase your ability to serve customers well."

6 *The Human Side of Quality*

THE MODEL of the quality company of the 1990s may not be a company at all in the business sense, but a small troupe of Australian performers who call themselves Circus Oz. Circus Oz is a truly magical organization, built on trust and mutual respect, in which each person is clearly responsible for the quality, creativity, and productivity of his or her own work . . . and involved and committed to the success of the enterprise as a whole.

Through its participative structure, the Oz company has solved the problem that bedevils so many American corporations today—how to do more with less; how to be the best—the "Greatest Show on Earth"—with limited resources.

The Oz solution is empowered and involves people. One moment a performer is catching his mates as they fly through the air with the greatest of ease; the next he is a trampoline expert, a jumping jester who always ends in an upright position. Another performer proves to be a gifted comedienne who is equally adept at fire-eating and scrambling to the top of a human pyramid. Everyone in the troupe, it seems, is a musician, clown, aerialist, and stagehand. All of the performers are actively involved in the design of their "work" as well as in the business side of the organization.

Through the mechanism of total involvement, the twelve members of Circus Oz somehow manage to convince audiences around the world that they are the proverbial cast of thousands. The illusion is powerful testimony to the positive things that can happen when people at all levels of an organization are empowered with the training, skills, and knowledge they need to do good work; are involved in the success of the organization; are rewarded and recognized for the quality of their efforts; perform in teams built on trust and respect; and communicate openly and honestly with each other.

Circus Oz offers a promising hint of what the quality corporation of the 1990s will be like. In the face of growing competition at home and abroad, quality-driven organizations are turning away from the authoritarian management practices of the past and focusing instead on their greatest potential asset—their people. Today, more and more companies—with the blessing and aid of labor unions—are creating work environments in which employees are able—and encouraged—to participate in decision making that will directly and indirectly affect their jobs.

The Japanese Paradigm

The postwar productivity movement in Japan is widely considered the impetus, and model, for the new participative-management approach. Lagging behind the rebuilding efforts of European countries and convinced that high productivity could serve as a cornerstone for quality improvement and economic growth, the country established the Japan Productivity Center in 1955 to spur a national movement to fully utilize the potential of its hardworking people.

Speaking at the International Productivity Symposium III in Washington in 1988, Masao Kamei, chairman of Sumitomo Electric Industries, said three features characterized the movement from the outset. First, management put people first. "It is the workers who actually make improvements and innovations, and no increase in productivity can be expected unless management treats workers with the greatest respect," he said.

Second, workers participate in corporate management. Third is the notion that the fruits of improved productivity must be shared among management, labor, and customers.[1]

While the commitment to the third point is debatable (given the minuscule size and gigantic cost of the average Japanese home, the absence of a good basic infrastructure—such as decent highways and sewage systems—and the highly inflated cost of farm and consumer goods, the average American might wonder exactly *who* is benefiting from improved productivity), there is no question that the emphasis on motivating people to do good work is a major factor in the Japanese miracle.

Although cultural differences would make transferring an exact replica of Japanese-style participative management to the United States impossible (even if it were desirable to do so), some of the basic assumptions identified by professor Tadao Kagono of Kobe University as the management "paradigm" used in many Japanese organizations have been successfully transplanted. These assumptions are:

- Management should rely on the wisdom of the people at the bottom of the organization.
- Motivation and commitment of the majority are more important than the motivation and commitment of a few.
- To motivate the majority, jobs must be secure and the differences in rewards minimized.
- To cope with change, the labor force should be flexible, job classifications should be minimal, and employees should have versatile skills.
- Information should be shared among the members of the organization.
- The implementation of a strategy is more important than its formulation.
- Employees are active participants in the organization, and they should, therefore, share its fruits.[2]

The Japanese paradigm encourages workers to make a full commitment to the company and to develop "company-specific" skills—the ability to work with peers, create people networks within the organization, and understand their jobs in an organizational context.

THE AMERICAN APPROACH

The American approach to workplace participation flies under many different banners—"participative management," "employee involvement," "total employee involvement," or "total quality management." Whatever it's called, the objective is the same: to motivate people to "work smarter," to be more productive, to do the right things right.

In some cases, such as Herman Miller and ServiceMaster, the movement to engage the hearts and minds of workers is simply part of the culture of the companies and is driven largely by the personal convictions of their leaders. As Max De Pree, former chairman of Herman Miller, the innovative Michigan furniture maker which has had a participative environment for more than forty years, said, "It begins with a belief in the potential of people. Participative management without convictions about the gifts people bring to organizations is a contradiction in terms."[3]

For others, the movement is less moral than pragmatic. It has become increasingly clear that the traditional methods of motivating employees do not work. As Frederick Herzberg pointed out in his brilliant 1968 *Harvard Business Review* article—the best-selling reprint in the magazine's history—such approaches as more money, fringe benefits, comfortable surroundings, sensitivity training, and talking about the big picture do not motivate people. These are simply factors that create dissatisfaction if they are absent; they do not make people feel good about their jobs or give them the needed internal generator.

What does? Herzberg said—correctly, we believe—that the keys are recognition of achievement, pride in doing a good job, more responsibility, advancement, and personal growth. In short, job enrichment. But how are these elusive factors produced?

The personal journey to improvement is just now getting some attention in America, and new ideas and research are proliferating. As always, the new thinking finds it tough to break in against conventional wisdom. In the field of quality, that "wisdom" is dominated by the Deming declaration that "85 percent of the problem is management" and all other theories are misdirected.

The "blame management" approach is good for the consulting businesses and is popular with unions—but it is a great disincentive to individuals. Not only does this popular proclamation fly in the face of the "seek no blame" tenet that the consultants advocate, but it *disproportionately* represents the proper and effective role for top management.

In new research findings, Harvard professor Michael Beer and his colleagues Russell A. Eisenstat and Bert Spector have found that "effective corporate renewal starts at the bottom, through informal efforts to solve business problems." In their research they discovered that effective change programs start not with corporate policy statements and the "vision thing" but at the periphery of the company, in a plant or division, under the leadership of a general manager focused on a specific business problem with individuals. Writing in the *Harvard Business Review,* they say:

> Most change programs don't work because they are guided by a theory of change that is fundamentally flawed. The common belief is that the place to begin is with the knowledge and attitudes of individuals. Changes in attitudes, the theory goes, lead to changes in individual behavior. And changes in individual behavior, repeated by many people, will result in organizational change. According to this model, change is like a conversion experience. Once people "get religion," changes in their behavior will surely follow.
>
> This theory gets the change process exactly backward. In fact, individual behavior is powerfully shaped by the organizational roles that people play. The most effective way to change behavior, therefore, is to put people into a new organizational context, which imposes new roles, responsibilities, and relationships on them.[4]

We submit that a significant part of the "new organizational context" Professor Beer and his colleagues call for is outlined in Chapter 9 in the description of AT&T's quality archetype study, which provides valuable insight into what motivates

Americans to do quality work. All that's required is the courage and willingness to experiment with this challenge.

Meanwhile many of the organizations we have studied have had success using a variety of employee involvement methods. These techniques tap the creative abilities of their employees for problem solving and continuous improvement, with benefits accruing to both the individual and the organization.

ENHANCING PERSONAL QUALITY

To win in a service business, a company has to concentrate on the outcome aspects of service. These aspects focus on reliability: whether you provide things in a timely, accurate manner; whether you keep your promises.

However, the things that will differentiate you as a high-quality provider of service are process-related. How you treat the customer is what distinguishes you from your competitor. This has to do with the empathy, with the assurance, with the willingness shown in your response to customers.

It was this conclusion that led MetLife, a pioneer in the use of research to identify and meet the concerns of customers, to develop a program aimed at the personalization of quality customer service.

Called Achieving Personal Quality—APQ, for short—the program began with research directed at both internal and external customers. The company used focus groups in which customers were asked to describe examples of good service and bad service. Out of about a hundred stories, MetLife identified a finite group of behaviors and classified them into what it calls the six attributes of personal quality. The six attributes are:

- treat the customer as you want to be treated when you are a customer
- take personal responsibility when you are a service provider
- improve yourself so you can improve service to the customer
- share your knowledge, skills, and time with others, both customers and co-workers

- have a positive outlook and be persistent in all of your dealings
- communicate effectively

"There's nothing earth-shattering or surprising about these attributes, says quality manager Mary M. LoSardo. "In fact, as we moved ahead in the development phase, we had no argument from anyone that we presented them to. But the question then becomes: if we all accept that these six attributes are at the heart of how customers want to be treated when they are looking for service, why don't we always receive this kind of treatment? Even more importantly, why don't we always deliver it? In other words, while it's easy to *identify* what customers *want,* it's not easy to *do* what customers want."

To help put APQ into action, MetLife hired Larry Miller, a consultant and author of *American Spirit: Visions of a New Corporate Culture,* to develop a seminar that focuses on what the company calls "the self-mastery cycle."

"The core of the cycle is a positive vision, a dream of what it is that we want to be," LoSardo says. "This is then broken down into specific goals, pinpointing the behaviors that will lead you to that positive vision. Identifying activators—things that will get you started and serve as clues to help you fall into 'good' habits—is the next part of the cycle. And, of course, you have to have tracking systems to know if you're making progress. When you are successful, you must reward yourself to reinforce the changes that are taking place. Finally, as you achieve one goal, you must look forward to the next. After all, the cycle is a wheel—and a wheel that only turns once doesn't get you very far."

To spread the message throughout the corporation, MetLife developed a series of videotapes, as well as an employee handbook that summarizes the material on the self-mastery cycle that appears in each tape, a personal development journal that encourages people to work on their own, applying the cycle to both work-related and non–work-related objectives, and a leader's guide for use in discussion groups.

"It's difficult to change work habits," LoSardo admits. "But, by enhancing our employees' interpersonal abilities, by improving their interactions with customers, by encouraging them to practice the personal quality attributes, we believe we can achieve a competitive advantage."

DRIVING OUT FEAR

Aside from W. Edwards Deming's eighth point (see Appendix B), "Drive out fear," not much has been said about fear in the workplace, an emotion that dominates the psyche of the typical American at work and has a crippling effect on quality and productivity.

Based on the first extensive research on fear in the workplace, Deming's point might better be stated in this way: Acknowledge fear in the workplace, create an environment that enables discussion of the "undiscussibles," value criticism by employees, create processes for addressing the causes of fear, don't shoot the messenger, support those who speak up.

Fear in corporate America takes many forms. Maybe the most insidious manifestation is "all the time people spend in meetings not saying what's really on their minds." These *silences,* say Kathleen D. Ryan and Daniel K. Oestreich, are built into organizations at all levels and have a profoundly debilitating effect on quality and productivity. In *Driving Fear Out of the Workplace: How to Overcome the Invisible Barriers to Quality, Productivity, and Innovation,* Ryan and Oestreich take a hard, straightforward look at this hidden barrier to improvement.

Their book is not about fear of change, fear of failure, or other familiar fears, but fear of speaking up—described by the authors as "a composite of many types of workplace anxieties, which together form a most basic human barrier to improving an organization." The authors discovered:

1. Fear of speaking up exists at *all* levels.
2. Seventy percent of employees do not speak up because of fear of repercussions.
3. There is basic mistrust between bosses and employees.
4. Most managers *unconsciously* threaten employees.

Surprisingly, the fear of speaking up has less to do with fear of losing a job (only 11 percent) than with losing face or credibility (27 percent). Employees don't want to be seen as troublemakers or boat rockers. They feel they cannot afford to be seen as not being a team player or as acting in an unprofessional way.

The consequences of this kind of fear are clear: negative feelings about the organization (reported by 27 percent) and negative feelings about oneself (reported by 19 percent). The authors list the negative impact on quality as follows:

Lack of extra effort
Making and hiding mistakes
Failure to meet deadlines and budgets
Loss of effective problem solving
Working on wrong priorities
Loss of creativity, innovation, and risk taking

The authors identify several sources of fear in the workplace. Among these is ambiguous behavior, which includes secretive decision making, uninviting behavior, lack of or indirect communication, and lack of responsiveness to suggestions. Also fear-producing is abrasive/abusive conduct: silence, glaring eye contact ("the look"), brevity or abruptness, snubbing or ignoring people, insults or put-downs, blaming or discrediting, an aggressive/controlling manner, threats about the job, yelling and shouting, and physical threats.

Eliminating fear in the workplace begins with a simple nonjudgmental acknowledgment that fear is present. This is easier said than done, but until fear in the workplace is addressed, all other management efforts at improvement will be correspondingly ineffective.[5]

LISTENING TO THE PEOPLE WHO ACTUALLY DO THE WORK

Many companies have found that involving workers in the design of new facilities contributes positively to employee "buy-in." Boeing used the participative approach throughout the construction of a new sheet metal fabrication plant in Auburn, Washington, using the skills and knowledge of its work force to help design the physical arrangements, organizational structure, and other cultural aspects of the new facility.

"The approach was based on the philosophy that 'people support what they help create,' " said Boeing chairman Frank Shrontz. "The new facility has many innovative features that came from an employee involvement process that began long before the first steel girder was erected."

In 1988, 250 employees of the previous sheet metal facility met for three days in the Local 751 International Association of Machinists and Aerospace Workers hall to learn about high-performance organizations and to draft original recommendations for the new center.

Their 4,500 recommendations were divided into twelve categories, such as job design, reward systems, recruitment and selection, and factory layout. Twelve groups of six employees each then began research, including reading material, discussions with experts, and visits to other high-performance organizations throughout the country.

The original ideas were then condensed to 142 recommendations, and when the new facility opened in June of 1990, many of them had been implemented. They included eliminating "status symbols" such as privileged parking, dress codes, and management/employee segregated eating facilities; a facility-wide no-smoking policy, and a joint union-management committee, with grass-roots representation, to deal with quality-of-work-life issues. Other recommendations representing departures from traditional labor agreements are still in the development and discussion stage.

The recommendations began to pay off almost immediately. Sheet metal parts have traditionally required an average flow time of forty working days, from the first step in the production process to the completed part. With the more modern and efficient operation in the new facility, flow time for the average part is four days, resulting in a major reduction in inventory, less floor space, and faster response to customers.

The Auburn experience is typical of the renewed emphasis on quality improvement at Boeing. A great deal of attention is being directed at improving the "human side" of the business. Managers are being trained in performance management that is geared to teaching them how to work with subordinates in setting individuals' goals and objectives. Workers' job descriptions are being rewritten to provide more accurate and understandable explanations of the actual responsibilities of the individual. Employees are being retrained for new jobs that require new technology or processes.

As Frank Shrontz put it: "Changing the 'people culture' of a company offers perhaps the biggest challenge and the best opportunity to enhance both productivity and quality. You can invest heavily in the best technology, but without a trained, motivated, and well-managed work force, no real gains are likely to be made."

FORMING TEAMS . . . TO SOLVE PROBLEMS

The old American competitiveness strategy was based on having an elite corps of executives manage organizations that mass-produced products at low cost, producing high profits. The new strategy is to build teams that design and continually improve the functioning of organizational processes, producing customer satisfaction.

The shift in emphasis is driven by convincing evidence that work teams improve quality and productivity because they foster greater employee involvement which, in turn, builds commitment to corporate success.

Work teams vary in focus and degree of autonomy from small informal groups assigned by management to solve specific short-term problems to permanent, completely "self-directed" teams, whose members possess a wide range of cross-functional skills and are given broad decision-making authority and access to the information they need to make good decisions.

In their book, *Self-Directed Work Teams—The New American Challenge,* a group of organizational experts associated with Zenger-Miller, an international training firm, defines self-directed work teams as ". . . a highly trained group of employees, from six to eighteen, on average, fully responsible for turning out a well-defined segment of finished work. . . . Work teams plan, set priorities, organize, coordinate with others, measure, and take corrective action—all once considered the exclusive province of supervisors and managers. They solve problems, schedule and assign work, and in many cases handle personnel issues like absenteeism or even team member selection and evaluation."[6]

Self-directed teams require a high level of management trust and commitment but they also offer the greatest potential return in improved quality, productivity, and employee morale. To be successful, the work team concept must be backed by a top-level commitment to provide the necessary resources and to protect the effort through its shaky infancy. For dozens of American companies the payoffs have been impressive.

But leadership is essential. "Work by teams will only be meaningful if it is informed and prioritized by managers who are working to improve the fundamental organizational systems. This means that, in fact, both the 'worker' and the 'manager' will be much more 'enabled and empowered' than ever before," says Bill Parr, director of the Center for Organizational Effectiveness at the University of Tennessee.

A few years ago senior executives at TRW Steering and Suspension, a pioneer in the use of work teams, were looking for ways to improve the methods of launching new products. The result of this internal self-analysis was the implementation of a cross-functional team approach called Managing for Reliability (MfR), which uses tools such as simultaneous engineering, project management, and proactive engineering techniques to meet customer and internal objectives when launching new products or establishing new manufacturing processes.

"The team focuses on the total program requirements instead of each function focusing on their small part," says John J. Knappenberger, formerly TRW's vice president of quality and current chairman of the American Society for Quality Control. "Performance is evaluated on both individual accomplishment and the accomplishment of team objectives."

The process begins with the formation of a team that includes representatives from sales, product engineering, purchasing, manufacturing engineering, quality, and other functional areas as needed. A mission statement is developed, approved by top management, and a top-level manager is appointed as team sponsor. The sponsor's role is to coach and advise the team and assist in resolving significant conflicts. Throughout the program, the team keeps top management up to date on the progress made toward meeting team objectives.

The team validates product and process designs through a variety of quality assessment tools and uses print reviews and design reviews between functional departments, suppliers, and the customer to resolve manufacturing and quality issues. It works on the assigned project until the product or process is in production and no significant issues remain. At that time, the team prepares a report assessing how well it performed against established targets and outlining its recommendations. This closeout report serves as both a formal self-assessment and a vehicle for continuous improvement of the product or manufacturing process, as well as the MfR process.

. . . TO SAVE MONEY

Working in teams not only gives workers a greater sense of pride and participation, it also encourages them to identify and solve many simple, money-wasting problems that, when added up, have an impact on the bottom line. At International Paper's chipyard in Vicksburg, Mississippi, a team wanted to eliminate the housekeeping and safety problems created by wood chips being strewn across the plant grounds. The team determined the root cause, developed four alternative solutions, selected the best one, and directed its implementation. As a result, chip spillage has been reduced from 683 to 32.5 tons per year and cleanup time has been decreased from two and a half hours a day to thirty minutes. Overall, a $20 investment resulted in a $13,000 annual savings, in addition to improving housekeeping and safety.

The logging and fiber supply shop team at International Paper's Vaughn, Oregon, plant improved its procedure for repairing hydraulic lines on heavy equipment by developing a hydraulic hose diagram for each piece of equipment. Now when hoses fail on a remote job, the operator simply identifies the hose by looking at the diagram and then calls the shop to tell the mechanic which hose to bring to repair the equipment.

The system eliminates extra trips between the repair site and the shop to get the correct hose. The $960 solution eliminates $11,800 in annual costs.

In addition to formal team participation, the company's quality improvement process—launched in 1984—also encourages informal problem-solving. For example, three employees at the Mobile, Alabama, paper mill, on their own initiative developed a computer program that automatically lets operators working on an order know exactly what quality control guidelines and customer preferences apply to that order. The notes include special concerns, requirements, and any prior complaints. The new system makes it easier for everyone, even newcomers, to produce exactly what the customer wants.

"More than ever before, we are involving employees in decision making," says Newland A. Lesko, staff vice president and director, quality management. "Data-gathering, the use of the formal problem-solving process, statistical analysis, and open communication have become the norm, not the exception, in most of the company's operations. People are participating on teams and offering individual contributions at a rate never before seen in the company, and the trend is growing. The change has not been easy or quick, but it is definitely having a beneficial effect on our corporation and on the individuals involved."

. . . to Purchase Equipment

Another positive outcome of teamwork is that it often allows companies to add to their own process capabilities. For many years, Goodyear's Stow Mold plant had gone outside to buy one of the essential parts used in its mold process because it was more cost-effective than doing it in-house.

"We had a group of people who believed that if we had a certain type of machine called a drill/mill/lathe we ought to be competitive in doing it ourselves," says plant manager Mike Dague, who coordinated the project. "We did an economic analysis that indicated that we would have a real good payoff from acquiring the machine and sold the budget to management on that basis."

A team of fourteen hourly and salaried employees—mainly the people who would operate the machine—was formed to develop specifications for the high-tech, precision milling machine that turns mold rings and drills holes all in one operation. Utilizing a key specifications matrix, the team determined that there were machines from five manufacturers—domestic and foreign—that had the potential to do the job required. Representatives of the team visited three companies to see various machines in a production environment. The team began its initial deliberations in late 1989 and made its final equipment-purchase recommendation earlier this year. Indications are that the new capability will save Goodyear about $600,000 a year.

"This was a complete departure from the way we had bought equipment for our plants in the past," says section head Dow O. Wolfe. "When it came time for capital purchases, several key people from management would make the decision. This was a way of bringing a whole new level of knowledge into the process."

The Stow experience is an example of the kind of commitment that former chairman Tom Barrett has said he's looking for in institutionalizing Goodyear's Total Quality Culture: "Today we're looking at the entire corporation and we're asking for far more than getting a little better. We're asking people to rethink their jobs—everyone's jobs—with the idea of building total quality into it, not just improving the quality."

BUILDING EMPLOYEE TRUST

How do you get workers to trust each other? How do you make the principles of teamwork meaningful? Classroom training is helpful, but there is a big gap between textbook learning and real-life experiences.

That's why Du Pont's Fibers Division, the company's largest chemical business ($5.97 billion in 1989), has taken its training outdoors through its Empowered Learning Teams program. All of the division's 20,000 employees, except for those with health problems, are required to participate in a rugged two-day Playing to Win seminar that is more boot camp than boutique learning.

Designed by Pecos River Learning Centers of Santa Fe, New Mexico, the program emphasizes learning through experience, in both outdoor and classroom activities, and teaches teamwork, leadership, communication, planning, and interpersonal skills.

In one exercise, for example, employees are hooked together in teams of three and asked to climb a forty-foot wall. Obviously, they can go only as high as the weakest member can go. Everyone has to be committed to reaching the top or the team doesn't make it. Other exercises involve climbing a thirty-foot pole and zipping down a 300-foot wire.

"It's a wonderful feeling to see people who think they can't do something being cheered on by their peers, breaking down their fears and reaching their goals," says James F. Kearns, who launched the program when he headed the division. "The point of the program is to create teams that are really empowered and continually improving."

Playing to Win seminars are held at Du Pont's five regional training centers around the country. The initial effort cost more than $23 million but Kearns believes it was worth it.

"People were skeptical at first, but the program caught on quickly when it became apparent that the seminars are a valuable experience," he says. An unsolicited interoffice memo tells the story from one long-time employee's perspective:

ELT is not about silly games—it's about people. People who are somehow transformed from limiting their focus to "me," to broadening it with even higher intensity to "we." It's about watching a young secretary struggle with her terror and literally stretch her capabilities to conquer the pole. It's about seventeen other team members who rejoiced in her accomplishment, some with moistened eyes, as she wept in sheer joy and relief over her victory. It's about individuals who combine their limited talents with almost unlimited abilities.

But most of all, ELT training is about choices. It's about choosing to accept who I am or what I am, or striving to be the best I can be. It's about working at a plant for thirty or thirty-five years and choosing to do just enough to get by or leaving a trail of excellence that virtually screams "I was there." And it's about each one of us accepting the possible demise of Textile Fibers or choosing to work together to overcome some rather formidable obstacles that none of us can conquer alone.

ASKING EMPLOYEES WHAT THEY THINK

The leading quality companies are open to new ideas. They emphasize openness and sharing of information, and their employees' opinions are important to them.

Federal Express has long been a pioneer in the use of "attitude surveys" to identify opportunities for improvement. For more than a decade, FedEx has been asking its employees their opinion of company management through an annual Survey Feedback Action (SFA).

A standard, anonymous questionnaire is given to all employees each spring, covering such issues as immediate leadership, corporate leadership, organizational identification, rewards, cooperation, job conditions, quality improvement, safety, and putting feedback into practice. Linking the survey to defined corporate goals and making it an annual event helps top executives track the response to management initiatives.

"We believe that customer satisfaction begins with employee satisfaction," says CEO Frederick W. Smith. "That is why we so strongly adhere to our People-Service-Profit philosophy. Simply stated, if we put our employees first, they will deliver impeccable service, and profit will be the natural outcome."[7]

To encourage ideas from its associates, which is what it calls its employees, Milliken & Co. instituted in 1988 a program called Opportunity for Improvement (OFI). In the first year, the company averaged only one-half a suggestion for improvement per worker. Then the company adopted the "24/72 rule," meaning that the person who received the OFI had to respond in writing within twenty-four hours and in seventy-two hours had to explain what action was to be taken. In 1990 the number of OFI's per associate averaged nineteen, for a total of 288,000 suggestions. Of those, 88 percent were implemented.

"If that seems like a lot, it is sobering to know that the average Japanese company received thirty such OFI's a year per employee," Milliken says. "And leading Japanese companies received fifty to 100. I suggest that such a process is the way to let our associates know we want their ideas to help us do a better job in the world."[8]

PROMOTING COOPERATIVE LABOR/MANAGEMENT INITIATIVES

The lesson of the 1980s for both management and labor has been that hanging together is preferable to hanging separately. This is particularly true in the automotive industry, which was hard hit by foreign competition, leading to a loss of jobs and market share in the early part of the decade. The days when management and labor could afford to meet only at contract time and trade insults and accusations across the table have passed. The result is a wave of joint labor/management initiatives designed to inspire teamwork, improve quality, enrich jobs, and increase competitiveness.

One of the most innovative of these is the General Motors Quality Network, a total quality process led jointly by union and management.

"Through the Quality Network, teams of employees are identifying the best operating methodologies and leadership practices in the business world, adapting them to a 'GM way' of doing business, and sharing that way with other operations throughout GM," says Robert C. Stempel, chairman and CEO. "We are creating a continuous learning environment for everyone . . . and that includes me."

Part of Stempel's learning experience, for example, is driving a different GM model or a competitor's car to work each week on a rotating basis and letting his engineers know his impressions.

"We are building the kind of environment where teamwork is encouraged and comes naturally," he says. "We are working with the idea that every process in the company can be improved. The result is higher quality and lower costs, which means greater value to the customer."

One of the best examples of the new spirit of cooperation in action is at the Buick-Oldsmobile-Cadillac plant in Lansing, where workers are organized into business units that operate like small businesses. Each employee is encouraged to be involved in such issues as safety, housekeeping, control of materials, uptime, schedules, and engineering. Many have been trained in statistical process control. Workers may even call suppliers when they have a complaint about their products.

At Buick City, teams have been using statistical methodologies to make process changes in how electrical systems are assembled. This has dramatically improved the final quality of the Buick LeSabre. The Quality Network has now developed a strategy called statistical methodology, and the lessons from Buick City are being incorporated into training programs at other GM locations.

At the truck assembly plant in Shreveport, Louisiana, and at the engine plant in Flint, workers have instituted a production material inventory system based on several Quality Network strategies that are now being put into place at plants everywhere. The result has been improved product quality, reduced inventory costs, and greater employee involvement.

New methods of doing things require a massive re-education program, and GM has spent more than $2 billion in worker training since 1982, at least $800 million of that administered jointly with its union, the United Auto Workers. More than 90 percent of GM's hourly work force has received training in how to work together in teams and how to work together more effectively. Indeed, the GM/UAW training program is the world's largest privately funded educational system.

"Quality doesn't result from hundreds of thousands of people doing their own thing," Stempel says. "All our people have to function as a team. A winning sports team is more than a few stars. On a winning team, all the members are playing their assigned positions to the best of their abilities."

Breaking Down the Barriers

One of the major challenges of employee involvement is to break down the barriers that prevent employees from doing good work. Robert J. Paluck, cofounder of Convex Computer Corp., the market leader in "minisupercomputers" (supercomputers that cost $1 million or less), has turned motivation into a high art.

Whether it is pouring fresh concrete each year on a back patio to let new employees record their footprints in the company's Walk of Fame, using Susan B. Anthony dollars enclosed in a treasure chest to hand out the quarterly profit-sharing money, divided equally among Convex's 1,200 employees, or holding his twice-yearly "How the game is played" seminar to keep everyone informed on what needs to be done to ensure the company's success, Paluck's methods are unconventional.

He even held a fair to make a mundane groundbreaking a special event. Before an expansion of the company's facility in Richardson, Texas, employees were given a large selection of spray paints to decorate a parking lot that was to be the new site. In addition to some creative artwork, the employees painted large representations of Convex's key competitors. On the morning of the groundbreaking, Paluck drove onto the site in a large piledriver, cheerfully dropping large, overripe watermelons onto his competitors' logos.

Paluck's methods appear to be working. Cofounded in 1982 by Paluck and Steve Wallach, the company's senior vice president of technology, Convex has become a leading supplier of supercomputers worldwide. The company posted record profits in 1989 of $11.7 million on record sales of $158.6 million, up from $6.1 million on revenue of $105.6 million in 1988.

"Success starts with the concept of giving the customer something he can't get from someone else—find a need and fill it," Paluck says. "It's very easy to say, but employees of the company are the only ones who are capable of pulling it off. So you put your efforts into building an environment that is conducive to letting them accomplish that goal."

Paluck believes that behavior in companies is driven by people's natural instincts to stake out territories, build fences, and aggressively protect their turf. His favorite expression is, "We can't let our hormones get to us." To dramatize his point, Paluck even uses slides of dogs lifting their legs to mark their territory during his "How the game is played" sessions.

"Setting up territories is in our hormones and we can't stop it, so you need to recognize that it exists and make Convex one territory," he says. "It's wonderful to vent this against your competition as opposed to venting it within the company."

Convex also does the conventional things right. New-product developers work directly with customers to make sure the company is understanding and meeting their requirements. It has a solid quality-assurance program and has installed a Just-in-Time inventory control system that has reduced cycle time and increased production efficiency. It measures customer satisfaction regularly, both through twice-yearly internal surveys and through third-party research services. During 1989, internal and external surveys consistently rated Convex best in the industry in customer satisfaction. Items rated include hardware reliability, software satisfaction, technical assistance follow-up, on-time assistance, and on-site service.

But it is Paluck's unconventional methods that draw the most attention. At Convex, everyone has the same size office because, in Paluck's words, "Everyone is a manager, you manage your own time—the only true asset one has is time."

There is Buf, the company's stuffed gorilla, which is passed by its previous custodian to the individual or department that has the most pressure to complete a job at any one time—symbolizing the group that has "the monkey on its back."

And there is the annual beach party with 200 tons of sand trucked in, Halloween costume parties, and a regular every-Friday-afternoon party in the company's lunch room. The payoff is a remarkably close-knit cadre of employees with a very low turnover rate.

Paluck believes work should be fun, but he is also a realist.

"All organizations within this company are not happily holding hands running off into the sunset," he says, "but I'm sure we have more holding hands and running off into the sunset than others, and that's all we have to do to be better than our competition."

RECOGNIZING AND REWARDING POSITIVE RESULTS

There is general agreement that one of the most important strategies in establishing a participative workplace is formal recognition of a job well done. At Moore, the leading maker of business forms, recognition has been raised to a high art through the annual SAM award competition, open to all employees of the company. Playing off the first name—and high standards—of Moore's founder, Samuel J. Moore, the SAM (Success at Moore) award is aimed at fostering a team approach to quality improvement through the solution of frequently recurring problems or the improvement of existing, but merely adequate, processes, products, or services.

"The SAM awards are an important part of our quality process," says Sandra S. Park, director, quality management. "They are awarded during our annual Quality Week, which brings people from all over the firm together for a week-long series of activities that combines training, quality planning, and celebration."

Any group of people can form a team to compete for the award; interdepartmental and cross-functional teams are especially encouraged. Entrants are judged on their use of problem-solving techniques and their applicability to other situations, creativity of the solution, cost reduction, and how well the solution meets the needs of internal and external customers.

Banc One, the Columbus, Ohio-based bank holding company, with fifty-two banks and 670 branches in six states, has a reward and recognition program with eight levels, ranging from the Chairman's Quality of Customer Service award for affiliates—based on the Malcolm Baldrige award criteria—to individual We Care awards and "Wittys," based on the company's Whatever It Takes corporate positioning campaign.

"Recognition is a vital element in getting people involved and participating fully in their work," says Charles A. Aubrey, Banc One's chief quality officer. "It is a simple, but powerful, message to say: 'Thank you for doing a good job.'"

The logic for creating programs that recognize and reward high-performing individuals and work teams is clear. Quality organizations understand that employees who feel appreciated work harder and produce better products and services for customers. Indeed, more than fifty years ago Western Electric's Hawthorne Works, conducting pioneering studies on the impact of work conditions on productivity, discovered the "Hawthorne Effect," which holds that simply having management pay attention—any kind of attention—to workers automatically increases productivity.

Recognition and rewards take many forms. Some of the more common are thank-you notes from management, formal recognition ceremonies, days off with pay, tickets to ball games, a write-up in the company newspaper, dinner with the CEO, and money, to name just a few.

The granddaddy of formal reward systems is gainsharing, which has existed in a variety of forms for more than fifty years. Sometimes known generically as the Scanlon plan (for Joseph Scanlon, the former cost accountant, steelworker, union official, and, finally, MIT lecturer who was instrumental in developing the concept), the term was actually coined by F. W. Taylor in 1886.

Gainsharing is generally made up of three components: a philosophy of cooperation, an employee involvement system, and a financial bonus. The bonus is determined by a calculation that measures the difference between expected costs and actual costs during a bonus period. A formula is used to determine the percentage that is shared with workers.

Interest in gainsharing has grown tremendously in the past decade as two more recent variations—the Rucker plan and Improshare—have risen in prominence and formal research has confirmed the direct relationship between pay and performance.

What motivator works best? In a 1990 American Society for Quality Control/Gallup poll, employees were asked to rate four ways to increase their sense of job satisfaction. Among the choices, "letting you do more to put your ideas into action" (33 percent) outranked "pay you more" (27 percent), "recognize" the effort more (19 percent), and "listening to your ideas for improvement" (17 percent).

Pay is clearly important. But if you combine "let me do more" (33 percent) with "listen to my ideas" (17 percent), then half of all employees are saying that job satisfaction will increase if you simply pay attention to their ideas.[9]

Among the leading quality companies there is honest, and significant, disagreement about whether rewards should be financial or nonfinancial.

For example, in addition to its CEO Quality Awards, which recognize outstanding achievement within the company, Motorola's nonexecutive U.S. employees have received bonus payments in recent years averaging between 3 percent and 4.5 percent of total payroll through the company's Participative Management Program.

Milliken, on the other hand, does not give financial rewards because "doing good things is part of the job, not separate." Instead, it favors such things as just saying thanks, personal letters from top officers, hero presentations, certificates, associate or team of the year awards, and a recognition center in each department.

Milliken also has a program of Pinnacle Awards for suppliers that excel in providing the company with superior products and services. Suppliers are graded on quality, delivery, value, and service, and those who earn ninety points or more are designated "world class" and receive the Pinnacle Award.

Xerox recognizes team efforts through awards such as the Team Excellence Award and Excellence in Customer Satisfaction. Individuals are recognized through the President's Award and the Xerox Achievement Award. More than 40 percent of these awards are initiated by peer nomination. Xerox employees also share in the company's achievements through gainsharing, profit sharing, and various other financial incentive programs.

"We have found that our people around the world thirst for the opportunity to be recognized by the CEO because it is almost better than money," says Motorola CEO George Fisher. "I would be the last to say it is better than money, but the recognition, the pat on the back, for really making major headway on quality and cycle time goals can't be underestimated, and that pat on the back has to come from the top."[10]

ENGAGING THE "FROZEN" MIDDLE

If you ask American Airlines CEO Robert L. Crandall to explain how his company became the leading U.S. carrier in terms of revenues and operating income while also becoming the airline cited most frequently by customers for the quality of its services, chances are he will say it goes back to a policy decision made in the late 1970s to work toward improving the traditionally adversarial relationship between labor and management.

"The airline business has historically had a strong military bent and developed as a rather rigid, procedures-based and confrontational workplace," Crandall says. "On top of that, the industry became heavily unionized. Very early in the deregulation process, we made a sustained, long-term effort to change that confrontational, noncooperative, nonparticipative environment into an environment based on trust and mutual respect."

Even before American launched its highly regarded Quality of Work Life Program in 1983, the airline had already put in place a series of initiatives designed to involve all workers—from baggage handlers to flight personnel to senior managers—in the process of improving service quality. Crandall has been highly visible in the effort, speaking directly to large groups of employees at annual conferences around the American system.

This approach was instrumental in helping American get labor costs under control in the early 1980s. Crandall was able to sell his unions on a two-tier wage system, since adopted by most other major carriers. Under the plan, new employees come in at lower wage scales and gradually work their way up to parity with long-time employees.

"My feeling is that it's not really a matter of being more cooperative," Crandall says. "It's a matter of trying to change the nature of the work environment so that it is far more participatory and far more communications-oriented. Through the years, it has become clear to us that the notion of continuous improvement of service quality—which is what our people had started out wanting to provide—can be used as a reinforcing vehicle in our efforts to change the nature of the relationship between management and our people."

Most quality and training professionals will tell you that the hardest group to reach with a message of change within a corporation are middle managers and front-line supervisors. In a recent initiative, American decided to confront the challenge head-on with an educational program it calls Committing to Leadership (CTL).

"CTL represents a recognition that we can't return to the days when management made all the decisions and other employees carried out those decisions," says Anne McNamara, senior vice president of administration and general counsel. "Those days are gone forever. Committing to Leadership training was designed to give the leaders of the company the skills to create the participative environment that our overall quality process—Quality of Work Life—demands."

At the end of 1990, all 14,000 of the airline's managers and supervisors had completed the week-long course, which focuses on such participative issues as empowerment, employee involvement, teamwork and problem solving, and communications. Training was conducted in North Dallas, not far from company headquarters, and senior company executives spent Thursday afternoons responding to questions from participants.

All told, American spent $15 million on the program. One quantifiable result has been a dramatic reduction in the number of complaints per customer, from 1.2 per 100,000 passengers in June 1989 to .46 per 100,000 in June 1990. That represents 38 complaints from 12 million passengers, the best record in the industry. McNamara believes the payback will be much bigger as more and more departments and stations integrate CTL concepts into the way they do business.

"No company today can survive without the active participation of its employees," she says. "CTL was initiated to help us establish an operating environment where trust, cooperation, open communications, and employee involvement are a way of life for everyone."

KEEPING THE FAITH

Herman Miller, Inc., has long enjoyed a reputation for being one of the most progressively managed companies in America. The Zeeland, Michigan-based maker of office furniture has had a participative management system—in which workers have a say in decisions and a share in the successes—for more than forty years. Most years the system has worked well, but in 1985 the company's commitment was put to the test.

A slump in the computer industry, a wave of discounting, and manufacturing and delivery problems with the company's then new Ethospace line combined to produce the first earnings decline in fourteen years. Unlike many other companies, which have abandoned participative approaches when times got hard, Herman Miller decided to stick to its principles. In so doing, it proved that such a policy can be a formidable weapon for overcoming problems.[11]

Miller's workers responded to the crisis in a variety of ways. They suggested ways to trim $12 million from its annual costs; the sales force developed a significant amount of new business in the banking and insurance industries, segments in which the company had not been strong; and employees came up with ideas to cut the delivery times for the Ethospace office system to eight weeks from twenty-two weeks. As a result of these initiatives, the company quickly rebounded to profitability.

"Many companies have given up on participative management when the heat was on," says Max O. De Pree, son of the founder, chairman and former CEO. "That is exactly the time you ought to depend upon it most. I think you have to believe some very difficult things to make it work for a long time. It is not a theoretical position to be adopted after reading a few journals. You have to believe in the potential of people. Participative management without a belief in that potential and without convictions about the gifts that people bring to organizations is a contradiction in terms."

Founded in 1905 as the Star Furniture Company, Max's father, D. J. De Pree, joined the company in 1909 and became its president in 1911. Four years later, his father-in-law, Herman Miller, helped De Pree buy majority control. In return De Pree gave the company its current name.

Following the crash of 1929, the company faced some hard choices. It could lower quality and prices, as other makers of traditional furniture had done. It could simply close shop. Or it could do something that no other furniture maker was doing. D. J. De Pree chose the latter route.

In 1931 he hired Gilbert Rohde, who had established a reputation for designing custom-made furniture in the modern idiom, to design a line of space-saving, multi-purpose furniture that Herman Miller could make without cutting quality or lowering prices excessively. This shift to modern design, which no other furniture manufacturer was using, was eventually to draw upon the talents of America's greatest furniture designers—Charles Eames, Alexander Girard, Isamu Noguchi—and establish Herman Miller as the premier manufacturer of contemporary furniture in the U.S.[12]

"We came to believe that faddish styles and early obsolescence were forms of design immorality, and that good design improves quality and reduces cost because it achieves long life," the elder De Pree wrote.[13]

Deeply religious, D. J. De Pree was also concerned about the state of labor and management relations. As Max De Pree puts it: "I think my father was concerned about the way people were being treated in companies. He felt that we were running the risk of developing a class of management and a separate class of labor and that couldn't possibly be good for us as a nation."

In 1949 D. J. De Pree and his older son, Hugh, attended a lecture in Grand Rapids by Dr. Carl F. Frost, a psychologist and disciple of Douglas McGregor, author of *The Human Side of Enterprise*. In Frost, they found the management techniques to give substance to their convictions. They engaged him as a consultant—a move that was to make Herman Miller a pioneer in participative management.

In 1950, at Frost's recommendation, the company adopted gainsharing to give all workers a chance to influence decisions and to let them have a piece of the action if their efforts paid off. Every Herman Miller employee receives a quarterly bonus based on various benchmarks, including cost-saving suggestions.

All employees, from the chairman on down, are organized into work teams. The team leader evaluates his employees every six months, and the employees then evaluate the leader. On the plant floor, teams elect representatives to caucuses that meet periodically with line supervisors to discuss production problems. Workers with grievances are allowed to bypass the supervisor and go to the next executive level if they think it is necessary.

A profit-sharing plan paid in stock means that all of Miller's

U.S. employees with more than a year of service are shareholders. Job-sharing and part-time jobs make it easier for parents to spend time with their children, and the company offers up to $2,500 to employees who adopt children. When a worker has a baby, the company gives the parents a collector's item: a Charles Eames rocker. One of the latest innovations is "silver parachutes" for all employees. In the event of a hostile takeover, plant workers who lose their jobs would receive big checks along with the executives.

When top managers look for key employees, they focus more on values and ability to get along with people than on résumés. For example, De Pree recruited Michele Hunt, a young black woman from the state's Department of Corrections, where she was training to be a prison warden. Now in charge of human resources at Herman Miller, she may be the only executive in the U.S. to hold the title "vice president for people."

PART III:

THE FUTURE

What Needs to Be Done

7 *Follow the Leaders*

AT THE beginning of the 1990s we can with some confidence identify a number of companies that have successfully undergone a quality revolution. They are veterans of a campaign that has had to overcome entrenched resistance, has certainly not been painless or quick, and clearly has no end. Our honor roll of the leading companies in the quality movement so far includes the winners of the Malcolm Baldrige National Quality Award as well as other as-yet-undecorated combatants.

The one characteristic that is common to all of these companies is strong leadership—a chief executive who leads the charge emboldened by an unshakable belief in quality. There are not nearly enough of these leaders because, at heart, a commitment to improve quality involves significant change throughout an organization—in the way that a company deals with its customers, suppliers, and employees. And change is difficult.

"The fact is, meaningful quality improvement begins with questions that only senior managers are in a position to ask . . . questions that cut against the grain of the status quo . . . questions that challenge traditional assumptions. . . . And questions that require significant resources and organization-wide commitment to address completely," says George H. Labovitz, president, Organizational Dynamics, Inc., a quality-consulting firm.

Today, Labovitz's statements seem obvious. But in American companies in the early 1980s—when a few senior executives first began to perceive quality improvement as a survival issue—such thinking was rare. For the most part, quality was still regarded simply as a "control" issue, focused on weeding out defects generated in the plant or back office and measuring the related costs. Senior management paid it little attention, opting instead to delegate the responsibility to a few quality control engineers or other specialists. But as MIT economist Lester Thurow so pointedly states it: "Management is responsible for quality control. If American products are shoddily built, then American management is shoddy."[1]

One of the great lessons of the quality revolution is that leadership is the most important ingredient for launching and sustaining a quality improvement process. If the top dog and his immediate poundmates don't believe in the process and behave accordingly, it won't happen. The great mystery, of course, is what is leadership, anyway?

To paraphrase leadership guru Warren Bennis paraphrasing Wallace Stevens, the great American poet and insurance executive: managers wear square hats and learn through training; leaders wear sombreros and opt for education. The point of this little conceit—which springs from a Stevens poem called "Six Significant Landscapes"—is that managers are rationalists who are trained to think in a linear way at a time in history when problems are rarely clearly defined and almost never linear. Leaders—the sombrero guys—are those who have been educated, in Stevens' words, to consider "rhomboids, cones, waving lines, ellipses. . . ." In short, leaders know how to think beyond the limits of a boxed, right-angle world.

The Forum Corporation, a training, consulting, and research firm which has conducted extensive ongoing research on leadership over the past twenty years, traces the need for a fundamentally new view of business leadership to three sources: changing organizational structures in the modern corporation; a new, more diverse work force with rising expectations, diminished institutional loyalties, and less reverence for authority; and the modern quality movement itself, which first took root in Japan. Long before quality and customer focus became buzz words in the West, the Japanese had concluded that innovation, the power to make decisions, and the ability to mobilize others must exist throughout the ranks of the organization. They reasoned that in a complex environment those closest to the process are best suited to make decisions and see them through.

By studying a number of quality companies, including the Baldrige Award winners, it is possible to identify specific management practices and behaviors that have helped them create a climate in which continuous improvement can flourish.

SET DEMANDING GOALS

Without exception, leaders of quality companies establish clear, results-oriented goals for continuous improvement, set priorities, and communicate their expectations clearly.

For example, what distinguishes Motorola's quality efforts from those of many other companies is not so much the specifics—which are familiar to most quality professionals—but the amazing depth, variety, and level of demand.

Heading the list is Six Sigma Quality, a statistical measure of variation from a desired result that translates into a target of no more than 3.4 defects per million products, customer service included. Sigma—the 18th letter of the Greek alphabet—refers to the number of standard deviations from the mean in any given statistically measurable process. The mean is the arithmetic average; the standard deviation is a measure of variation from that average. The quality of most manufacturing processes in the United States is plus or minus three sigma, which means that there are 66,810 defects per million opportunities for error.

All Motorola departments, including those not directly involved in manufacturing parts, now have their own plans for reaching Six Sigma by 1992. That means designing products and developing manufacturing processes that will produce virtually zero defects. The company estimates that it saved $500 million in 1990 by reducing defects under the Six Sigma effort, which has now been adopted by Digital, IBM, Corning, Boeing, and others.

Motorola is taking its suppliers with it on the route to 99.9

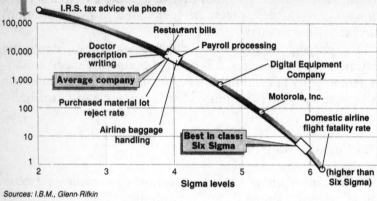

On the Road to Six Sigma
Number of defects per million units or steps.

I.R.S. tax advice via phone
Restaurant bills
Doctor prescription writing
Payroll processing
Average company
Digital Equipment Company
Purchased material lot reject rate
Motorola, Inc.
Airline baggage handling
Domestic airline flight fatality rate
Best in class: Six Sigma

Sigma levels (higher than Six Sigma)

Sources: I.B.M., Glenn Rifkin

percent perfection. Those who don't measure up are dumped. Six years ago the communications sector had 5,000 suppliers; now it has 1,600 and eventually it will have 400. The company is requiring all its suppliers to apply for the National Quality Award. One supplier was quoted in a *Fortune* article as saying: "If you can supply Motorola, you can supply God."

Another vital quality initiative is aimed at reducing "total cycle time"—the time from when a customer places an order until it is delivered. The company has even taken this concept into new-product development, where the clock starts ticking the moment the product is conceived.

The advantages of reducing total cycle time are many and compelling. First, it allows companies to deliver products that are closer to the customer's real-time requirements; they don't have to project consumer preferences an extra two or three years into the future. Second, shorter development times allow a company time to develop more products or enhance existing products to meet shifting tastes. Third, speeding up the process provides valuable experience and a sense of mission for a company's engineers and workers.

Motorola provides a textbook example of the value of time-based competition. A few years ago, everyone at the company assumed that it took three to five years to get a new electronics product from the drawing board to the marketplace. But when engineers at the Boynton Beach plant set out in 1986 to build a new paging device, they deliberately cut the best-case scenario in half. They realized that their only hope of meeting the eighteen-month timetable was to gather in as much "off-the-shelf" manufacturing technology as they could. Project managers fanned out around the world looking for the best legally available manufacturing technology. The effort took on the humorous, and accurate, name "Operation Bandit."

The twenty-four-person Bandit team, which included product design engineers, process developers, tooling designers, software specialists, as well as marketing and financial people, borrowed JIT ideas from Honda, advanced robotics techniques from Seiko, and computer-integrated manufacturing (CIM) techniques from other Motorola factories.

A list of the ideas incorporated into the new plant reads like a CEO's wish list of advanced competitiveness techniques: "benchmarking" (picking the best of the best techniques); "simultaneous engineering" (designing the product and the manufacturing systems simultaneously); "design for manufacturability and assembly" (reducing the number of parts and simplifying assembly, a technique developed by English engineer Geoffrey Boothroyd in the 1970s that has become increasingly important since a product's design fixes between 70 percent and 95 percent of its manufacturing costs); "flexible manufacturing" (every pager made must have different characteristics so that all customers in one area are not "beeped" at the same time); and "supplier reduction" (twenty-two suppliers were selected out of 300 potential companies).

The result of this effort is a superfast robotic production line that is state-of-the-art in flexible manufacturing. Two hours after an order is entered into computers in Schaumburg, Illinois, a customized pager comes off the line in Boynton Beach. The whole procedure—deploying the robots, gathering the supplies, assembling, inspecting, and packaging the final product—is managed by computers.

WALK THE TALK

In the parlance of quality professionals, "walking the talk" is the modern-day version of "actions speak louder than words." It means, quite simply, that in order to enlist the support of workers throughout a company for continuous improvement, management must do more than say it is committed to quality; it must do things that prove it. That means that leaders must make a personal, and visible, investment of time and effort.

One day Rosemarie Greco, then president of Fidelity Bank, stopped for gas at a service station in Philadelphia. The station's owner recognized the name on her credit card and told her he was applying for a loan at Fidelity but didn't quite understand the terms and conditions. When he explained the conditions, Greco confessed that she didn't understand them either. The next morning, she talked to the loan officer, got the gas station owner on a conference call, and went over the terms line-by-line.

Since Milliken launched its quality process in 1980, it has had a monthly meeting at which senior managers of the company spend the first four hours of the day—without fail—discussing the company's quality process, its measurement, and its evolution. The meeting has never been canceled.

When Xerox launched its Leadership Through Excellence program in 1984, it used a "cascading" style of training. The first person to complete training was David Kearns, who then taught his direct reports, and so on—all the way down to the shop floor.

At Wallace Co., a family-owned distributor of piles, valves, and fittings to the oil and chemical industries and winner of the 1990 Baldrige Award in the small-business category, each of the company's five top leaders has attended more than 200 hours of quality training since the Houston-based firm launched its continuous improvement process in 1985.

"A member of senior leadership is always present when any of our 280 associates are receiving training—for quality or for job skills—in order to deliver the message, 'This is important,'" says John W. Wallace, chief executive officer.

In total, Wallace—which had 1990 sales of about $90 million—has invested more than $700,000 and 19,000 hours of training and education in its work force. The results are impressive. Wallace's market share has nearly doubled from 10 percent to 18 percent in three years; it has formed long-term supplier relationships with customers like Union Carbide, Monsanto, and Dow Chemical; customer complaints have more than halved—from 36 in 1987 to 14 in 1989; on-time delivery has risen from 75 percent in 1987 to well over 92 percent in 1990 (the company's goal is 99 percent on-time by January 1, 1993); and sales per associate average $294,000 —$58,000 above the industry average.

ENCOURAGE OPEN COMMUNICATIONS

When the winners of the first Malcolm Baldrige National Quality Awards were announced in November 1988, few quality professionals were surprised that Motorola or Westinghouse's Commercial Nuclear Fuel Division were on the list. Both have long-established and respected quality improvement programs.

The real surprise was the third winner—Globe Metallurgical, a tiny Ohio-based manufacturer of ferroalloys. A sign of the times is the fact that Globe, with sales of about $120 million, two plants (one in Beverly, Ohio, and another in Selma, Alabama), and 210 employees, is the largest producer of silicon metal in the United States. Once a thriving industry, the ferrosilicon and silicon metal industries have shrunk significantly since the 1960s, with many U.S. producers dropping out because they couldn't compete with low-cost imports from Canada, Brazil, and Argentina. Imports now account for more than one-half of the silicon-based alloy sales in the United States.

Globe produces more than 120 different products in numerous size ranges, and its major customers include General Motors, Ford, and Dow Corning. Its products are sold through an outside sales agent, Pickands, Mather and Company, which has handled Globe's alloys exclusively since 1956.

When Arden Sims, Globe's president, Ken Leach, vice president—administration, and other young managers took over the direction of the company in 1985, their most pressing problem was to break down the barriers of mistrust between management and workers that had built up over the previous twenty years, particularly at the Beverly plant.

"The old management utilized an autocratic style, and the employees were considered little more than the machines they operated," Leach says. "Besides leading to labor problems, the employees were totally complacent about improving the operation."

In 1986 quality circle teams in four formats—departmental, interdepartmental, project, and interplant—were begun at each of Globe's plants. Each department team is composed of seven hourly workers—chaired by an hourly employee who is a team leader trained to maintain the focus of the group—and they meet weekly, before or after their regular shift, to discuss improvements unique to their department. Workers are paid overtime for attendance.

The team leader then sits in on the daily QEC (Quality-Efficiency-Cost) meeting where each suggestion is read aloud. The QEC Committee makes an immediate recommendation, and the plant manager has extensive authority to implement ideas quickly without further approval.

While the new quality system was being developed, the new managers were fighting for survival on several levels. The company's owner—Moore McCormack Resources—was looking to get out of the metals business in the wake of the bankruptcy of LTV, its biggest customer. In addition, the hourly work force at the Beverly plant was organized by the United Steelworkers of America. The union environment at the plant was very restrictive concerning work rules and manpower allocation. As a result, the size of the work force was much larger than the company could profitably sustain.

"As we began in 1985 to improve the company-union relationship and to elicit ideas from the hourly employees, our efforts were met with distrust," Leach says. "Employees who were willing to give ideas to the company to improve quality, efficiency, or cost, were looked upon as traitors to the union cause."

Through improved communications, the company sought to break down these barriers, and although the process was slow, employees began to change their attitude and many ideas began to flow. Then, in October 1986, a strike was begun at the Beverly plant which lasted a year and resulted in decertification of the union. In the meantime, Leach, Sims, and two other managers had organized a leveraged buyout of the company, which was completed in 1987.

"Many employees have now been recalled to work and have readily adapted to the new methods of work without the restrictive work rules," Leach says. "In an effort to further improve the work atmosphere, hourly employees now enjoy the same benefit and pension package as salaried employees, time clocks have been removed, and a profit-sharing program has been installed which is very lucrative for the employees, with the average employee receiving more than $5,000 a year in profit-sharing bonuses."

As a Baldrige winner, Globe has become a model of how employee involvement and a formal quality improvement process can be used as catalysts to turn around a troubled company in a troubled industry. Ironically, Globe entered the Baldrige competition more or less on a lark. Leach got a copy of the application a few days before the deadline and spent a weekend filling out the forms.

DELIVER ON YOUR PROMISES

When your business is moving a million-and-a-half high-priority packages a day, and you've guaranteed that they will "absolutely, positively" arrive overnight, you had better have people and procedures in place that assure that you can deliver on your promise. For 1990 Baldrige Award winner Federal Express, reliability is its major source of competitive advantage, and continuous improvement is a way of life within the company.

"Our business is totally customer service," says James L. Barksdale, executive vice president and chief operating officer. "Consequently, we have developed highly sophisticated systems of measurement and reward that force us to focus on the customer. Every package we deliver is critically important to some customer and we try to communicate this idea to all of our 94,000 employees worldwide. It's hard work and it's continuous, but there's simply no other way for us to survive and prosper."

Since it was conceived and launched by chairman and chief executive officer Frederick W. Smith in 1973, Federal Express has rapidly grown into the leading air freight company in the world, with more than $6 billion in annual revenues. The company picks up and delivers more than 1.5 million packages a day, all of which must be tracked in a central information system, sorted quickly at facilities in Memphis, Indianapolis, Newark, Oakland, Los Angeles, Anchorage, and Brussels, and delivered to customers, usually before 10:30 A.M. on the following day. The firm's air cargo fleet of more than 100 Boeing 727s, 6 DC-8s, and 170 Cessna 208s is now the world's largest.

In an operation that large and that complex, there are plenty of opportunities for things to go wrong. More than 250 planes a day must take off and land on schedule. Ground operations have to work like clockwork. Tracking and billing of shipments must be accurate. Competition in the air freight delivery business is intense, and any level of performance less than perfection means a potential lost customer. On this score, FedEx's stated quality goals are unequivocal: 100 percent on-time deliveries; 100-percent-accurate information on every shipment to and from locations throughout the world; and 100 percent customer satisfaction.

"Only totally engaged and committed people can produce the level of daily performance that Federal Express has achieved," says Osvald Bjelland, a leading European consultant on workplace productivity who works frequently with Scandinavian Airlines on quality and performance issues. "That commitment can't be bought; it can't be directed; it can't be 'controlled' in the classic manufacturing sense. It can only be won over a period of time by consistent and enlightened leadership on the part of management."

Fred Smith obviously agrees. In accepting the Baldrige Award on behalf of Federal Express employees, he said: "In a service company, the customer's perception of quality is held in the hands of its people. Each daily interaction can be priceless or disastrous. It is this human side of quality that is so often the only side of service our customers see. We believe that customer satisfaction begins with employee satisfaction. That is why we so strongly adhere to our People-Service-Profit philosophy. Simply stated, if we put our employees first, they will deliver impeccable service, and profit will be the natural outcome."

Consistently rated as one of the best places to work in America, Federal Express has a "no layoff" philosophy and its Guaranteed Fair Treatment (GFT) grievance process is used as a benchmark by firms in many industries. The company has a generous profit-sharing program, flextime provisions for clerical workers, and a tuition reimbursement program. Some 20 percent of the company is owned by employees.

Clearly, the company's reputation for reliability and quality service is rooted in its philosophy of putting people first and treating them well.

To spur progress toward its ultimate target of 100 percent customer satisfaction, Federal Express replaced its old measure of quality performance—percent of on-time deliveries—with a twelve-component index that comprehensively describes how its performance is viewed by customers. The program is called Service Quality Indicator (SQI). Six of the twelve components originated in the company's complaint-handling program, known internally as the "hierarchy of horrors." The focus is important since the best estimates are that only about 30 percent of customers who are dissatisfied will ever tell the seller about it.

Several of the components deal with failures that the customer sees directly, such as late delivery, damaged packages, invoices missing proof of delivery information, and abandoned calls. Other categories that the customer doesn't see are such things as aircraft delays in minutes. Each of these occurrences is measured daily and treated as at least one failure point. The more severe problems are weighted in proportion to their negative impact on customers. For example, each damaged or permanently lost package is weighted by a factor of 10. If a package is five minutes late, that's a 1; if it's a day late, that's a 5.

The twelve categories are totaled to give an average daily failure point score, which is reported weekly to the entire company. The goal is to have fewer average daily failure points at the end of each year than there were at the end of the previous year. This measurement is the company's only service objective under its Management-by-Objectives (MBO) program, with the five-year objective to have only one-tenth of the average daily failures that occurred at the beginning of year one.

As a way of putting teeth into the SQI program, no one in management—line or staff—receives any bonus money from the MBO program if the goal has not been met at the end of the year. In addition, there is a vice president in charge of a cross-functional team for each of the twelve components who has to present his or her team's progress in front of senior management every ninety days. During the first year of the program, the absolute number of failures was reduced by 12 percent despite a 20 percent growth rate in volume of business.

"Every failure we avoid means less money returned under our guarantee, fewer packages that have to be expedited on commercial airlines and, most important, a satisfied customer, which usually equates to at least keeping the revenue already being generated from that customer," says John R. West, assistant to the chief operating officer.

In addition to involved employees and a tough measurement system, technology plays a key role in Federal Express' ability to deliver reliable, high-quality service. Recognizing that customers choose air express companies as much for their one-courier shipment control as for their speed, the company began developing its innovative COSMOS package tracking system in the late 1970s and has been refining it ever since.

The heart of the system is the SuperTracker, a hand-held computer used for scanning a shipment's bar code every time a package changes hands between pickup and delivery. This information in turn is instantly transmitted via a mobile terminal mounted in the courier's van to a "Smart Base" computer where it can be accessed by any of the company's customer service agents nationwide. This allows the agent to tell a customer exactly where his package is at any point in the "life" of the delivery.

"People, measurement, and communication—these are the principles upon which we've built our reputation for quality service," says John West. "They may not be the traditional approaches to total quality management but I sincerely believe they are the keys to achievements we made in quality and service."

MEASURE YOUR COMPANY AGAINST THE BEST

You can't be a winner if you don't know the score. Leaders use formal measures to see how they are doing, in terms of both internal improvements and customer satisfaction. They regularly benchmark their company's performance against that of others.

One of the most powerful weapons in the arsenal of Xerox's Business Products & Systems business—winner of a 1989 Baldrige Award—is its Customer Satisfaction Measurement System, which for the past ten years has been surveying some 200,000 Xerox customers a year to identify major areas of dissatisfaction and address their root causes. The company uses the information generated by the system—perhaps the best inside or outside the copier industry—to develop concrete business plans with measurable targets for achieving quality improvements necessary to meet customer needs.

"Out of this effort we have designed a number of customer-focus initiatives," says Peter Waasdorp, manager of the Customer Satisfaction Program office. "One of the most important things we've done is to empower each of our sixty-three districts to directly meet the needs of customers instead of pushing problems along to the regional or headquarters level. Our goal is to resolve 95 percent of all customer concerns within two days."

Other customer-driven programs to come out of the measurement system include efforts to reduce the number of pricing plans and simplify terms and conditions; differentiate and individually serve the needs of different-sized businesses; use information technology to improve the dispatching of service and parts; use on-line interactive telecommunications to monitor large machines and anticipate problems before they happen; achieve "faultless installation" with the goal of having 100 percent of all deliveries be perfect; and better manage inventories.

The payoff, as reported in the company's Baldrige application: highly satisfied customers have increased 38 percent and 39 percent for copier/duplicator and printing systems respectively; customer complaints to the president's office have declined more than 60 percent; customer satisfaction with Xerox sales processes has improved 40 percent; service processes, 18 percent, and administrative processes, 21 percent.

Xerox also pioneered the use of benchmarking as a competitive strategy—that is, studying the best in the world at a particular function and adopting that approach as the standard. Today, Xerox formally defines benchmarking as: the continuous process of measuring products, services, and practices against the company's toughest competitors and against companies recognized as industry leaders. The amount of benchmarking Xerox does has increased dramatically since 1984: from 14 performance elements benchmarked to nearly 240 today. The ultimate target for each attribute is the level of performance achieved by the world leader, regardless of industry.

Benchmarking teams, which can consist of up to twelve employees, work independently at their own schedules. Investigations take from nine to twelve months and may involve three to six different companies.

Over the past decade, the list of companies Xerox has benchmarked has grown to include the names of some of America's most successful corporations, including American Express (billing and collection); American Hospital Supply (automated inventory control); Ford (manufacturing floor layout); General Electric (robotics); L.L. Bean, Hershey Foods, and Mary Kay Cosmetics (warehousing and distribution); Westinghouse (Baldrige Award application process, warehouse controls, bar coding); and Florida Power & Light (quality process).

The benchmark for meeting daily production schedules is the near-perfect record achieved by Cummins Engine Company, a goal that resulted in a Xerox schedule improvement of 75 percent. The company's benchmarking of L.L. Bean's warehouse operations contributed 3 to 5 percent of an overall 10 percent productivity gain in warehousing and materials handling.

How Xerox Does Benchmarking

With more than a decade of experience in benchmarking, Xerox has developed a ten-step model that is used by all departments that want to do benchmarking studies. The steps are:

1. *Identify what is to be benchmarked.* A team selects a product, a service, a process or a practice, or even a level of customer satisfaction. The goal is to determine whether the area of interest is managed in the best possible way.

2. *Identify comparative companies.* Benchmarking partners can be other operating units within the company, competitors, or noncompetitors who are judged to be the leaders in the area being benchmarked.

3. *Determine data collection method and collect data.* In true "apples-to-apples" fashion, teams determine what measurements will be used in the benchmarking process. Then a trip is often made to the selected company, and face-to-face exchanges are conducted with principals in both firms. Often, a tour of the benchmarked area is included.

4. *Determine current performance levels.* Once the team has gathered the necessary data and compared it with current performance levels, the results are analyzed. Generally, they reveal a negative or positive performance gap. Sometimes they show no significant differences.

5. *Determine future performance levels.* The benchmarking team forecasts the expected improvements by the company under study for use in establishing new goals. This assures that goals will still equal or perhaps exceed the performance of the studied organization following the time it takes to implement the team's findings.

6. *Communicate benchmark findings and gain acceptance.* The team presents its methodology, findings, and proposed strategies to senior management. This information is also communicated to the employees who will be asked to help implement the new strategies.

7. *Establish functional goals.* After concurrence, the team presents final recommendations on ways in which the organization must change, based on the benchmark findings, to reach the new goals.

8. *Develop action plans*. The team develops specific action plans for each objective that provide for behavioral considerations in implementing change with strategies for obtaining full organizational support.

9. *Implement specific actions and monitor progress*. The plans are put into place. Data on the new level of performance are collected. Adjustments to the process are made if the goals are not being met, and problem-solving teams may be formed to investigate.

10. *Recalibrate benchmarks*. Over time, the benchmarks are re-evaluated and updated to ensure that they are based on the latest performance data.

MONITOR CUSTOMER SATISFACTION

Customer satisfaction measurement plays a key role at Westinghouse's Commercial Nuclear Fuel Division, winner of the 1988 Baldrige Award. The division maintains close—usually daily—contact with its utility customers and regularly collects technical data to evaluate the performance of its fuel assemblies. Quality-oriented customer service plans have been developed for each individual customer, and these plans are jointly reviewed each quarter.

In 1988 the division established a quantitative system for measuring customer satisfaction, including such factors as project engineering, sales management, and field sales. These ratings are reviewed and benchmarked by customers, and the information is shared throughout the organization—marketing, engineering, manufacturing—to establish an action plan for improving the division's rating.

Joint quality teams have been formed with a number of utility customers, and customers are increasingly involved in the design of products. CNFD established a Fuel Users Group to provide feedback, explore ways to enhance fuel performance, and even to design new products.

Like all of Westinghouse's business units, CNFD uses the Westinghouse Total Quality model developed by the company's highly regarded Productivity and Quality Center. Opened more than a decade ago, the center was the first corporate-sponsored resource devoted to quality improvement, and its 130 computer gurus, consultants, and engineers are dedicated—in the words of Quality Center marketing manager Carl Arendt—"to helping the company's business units do the right things right the first time."

Any business unit can ask the Quality Center to perform a Total Quality Fitness Review for all or part of its operations. More than 100 such requests are issued each year. The center then sends out a team that conducts interviews and analyzes them in order to identify weaknesses in training, processes, and products. Most importantly, the team surveys customers. Once the review is completed, the unit manager gets a Total Quality scorecard. The results are not passed up the chain of command; instead, the review team helps managers set up teams, deploy improvements, and measure results.

The Westinghouse Total Quality Model, developed by the Quality Center, states simply that if you want to be a total quality organization you must have quality management systems, quality products and technology, and quality people— and that the combined energies of your management, products, and people must be focused on customer satisfaction. The Total Quality model is also subdivided into twelve Conditions for Excellence, and today the company has programs in place to improve quality, on a continuous basis, in every segment of the organization.

BE THE "BEST-COST" SUPPLIER

Executives of Emerson Electric Co., the $7 billion–plus maker of electrical, electromechanical, and electronic products, do not crisscross the nation giving speeches on quality. In fact, CEO Chuck Knight grants few interviews, and the company has no "quality" department per se. Still, Emerson's reputation for product quality is unquestioned.

For example, Emerson produces electric clothes-dryer motors for the appliance industry with defects of less than 100 parts per million. That's close to Six Sigma quality. Emerson garbage disposers made for Sears have for ten years had the lowest rate of failure of any appliance item sold by that chain. Emerson compressors have one of the lowest failure rates of any residential air-conditioning compressor in the world.

How does Emerson do it? By focusing on market leadership and being the "best-cost" supplier. Knight will accept nothing less than being best-cost, meaning the lowest cost at a differentiated-quality level.

In Knight's view, the best-cost producer by defintion has the highest quality, including the best product performance. It's a given. Poor product performance is so costly that a best-cost producer must, in his words, "be committed to the very highest standards of quality." As Knight sees it, quality is a cost reduction, not a cost.

Emerson's best-cost-producer strategy, formalized and announced in the company's 1984 annual report, has six basic elements: dedication to quality; knowledge of the competitor; focused manufacturing strategy; formalized cost-reduction programs; effective employee communication process; and commitment to capital expenditures.

The key element of the strategy is simple and effective: find out your competitor's cost at a given level of quality and beat them. Emerson analyzes its competitors' costs in great detail, including costs of materials, processes, and overhead.

The company's approach to its 70,000 employees located thoughout forty division is to build and maintain an environment that is receptive to change. Managers are expected to be involved, set priorities, be tough—but fair—in dealing with people, establish and demand high standards, and encourage innovation.

Knight says that "quality, or whatever you call it, is a fad unless the person on the shop floor understands its impact on the company." This understanding must be acknowledged not just with a nod of the head but with words that can explain how his or her activity is tied to the performance of the company. Each employee must understand who the "enemy" (competitor) is, what the competitive pressures are, what the economics of his job are, and what cost reduction they are working on.

Cost reduction is serious business at Emerson. Programs are formalized, and each manager must be committed to this process. By commitment, Knight does not mean "an effort that is implemented only when times get tough." The process of cost reduction/productivity improvement is a basic part of the management and planning process at all times that yields "better results in good times than in bad."

Even the rather elusive business of communications is precisely defined at Emerson. Communications are directed to targets, programs, ideas, and schedules that take place at all levels of the company. It is the responsibility of communications to ensure that cost reduction is a "way of life" for every member of the company.

Knight believes that the best-cost-producer strategy requires a major commitment to capital expenditures. Such spending requires careful planning to "ensure that the competitive positioning of our product can be maintained," he says.

Each element of the company's strategy has a "guru" within the highest ranks of management, and every such individual has operations experience. Knight says he tried every conceivable kind of quality consultant, some of whom were a "complete waste of time." Now, under the Emerson system each best-cost-producer element has an in-house expert who is available to every operating unit. Requiring each guru to have operations experience (also a Japanese condition for management) keeps the element focused and practical.

The driver or incentive to make each of these elements work is not solely financial: It is basic to business. Said another way, financial incentives and compensation are tied to results from the elements of the strategy, not to the elements themselves.

Where has this strategy gotten Emerson? The company is number one or two in 86 percent of the domestic markets it serves. It has enjoyed thirty-three consecutive years of increased earnings per share and thirty-four consecutive years of increased dividends per share. During the American quality crisis decade of the 1980s, Emerson had a compounded annualized growth rate in earnings per share of 9.1 percent, more than double the 4.0 percent for the Standard & Poor's 500; return on equity averaged 19.2 percent; engineering and development expenses grew at an annualized rate of 13 percent.

Few "quality" companies can match that level of performance.

BEHIND EVERY LEADING ORGANIZATION THERE'S A LEADER

In popular American mythology, leaders are usually pictured as heroic figures. General MacArthur, his ever-present corncob pipe clamped between his teeth, wading ashore in the Philippines to make good on his "I shall return" promise is an image etched indelibly on the American unconscious. But, in truth, leadership in quality companies seems less a matter of style and charisma than a set of observable—and learnable—behaviors.

The Forum Corporation's research discovered that leadership in quality-oriented, customer-focused companies had less to do with individualism than with the ability to build and maintain relationships across the organization.

This is not to say that top-level symbolism is unimportant. Leaders of quality companies must make their commitment to continuous improvement visible, both to their own people and to the outside world. Before they decided to pursue the Baldrige Award, Roger Milliken and Fred Smith were among the least accessible executives in America to the media. Both overcame their reluctance in the service of the larger good—promoting quality improvement in American industry.

General Motors' quality improvement drive was limited by Roger Smith's lack of identification with the effort and his preoccupation with technological retooling. Smith delegated quality responsibilities to the GM president, breaking a cardinal rule of quality leadership. But, as many of Smith's unconventional (and unpopular) actions have turned out, this one was a blessing in disguise. In former president James McDonald and his successor, Robert Stempel, now CEO, GM had truly committed quality leadership at the top.

As the Roger Smith illustration makes clear, not all chief executives immediately buy into continuous improvement. Procter & Gamble's chairman Edwin L. Artzt admits that when he first heard that P&G was thinking of adopting total quality, he was skeptical.

"We already had more programs than a dog has fleas. What little I had read about total quality was full of jargon and buzz words, and the flow charts looked like the wiring diagram for my refrigerator," he says. "Besides, we were doing pretty good without this stuff. So I was a hard man to convince, but I have become a real convert to total quality, and I endorse it one hundred percent. Why? Because it works, when used intelligently, to help our company achieve clearly focused business objectives."

Continuous improvement has begun to make converts in government also. The most vocal supporter of quality on Capitol Hill is Pennsylvania Congressman Don Ritter, who has introduced legislation to establish national quality goals for American business, education, and government. The Quality Council created by Ritter's amendment would set quality goals, then ask that companies, unions, associations, and units of government make strong commitments to achieving these objectives. It would also conduct an annual White House Conference on Quality in the American Workplace that would bring together national leaders from business, labor, education, professional societies, the media, government and politics to address quality as a means to improve U.S. competitiveness.

"We're finally realizing that the real bulk of our competitors' successes is due to their commitment to quality, to 'do the right things right the first time,'" Ritter says. "Meanwhile, here in America, because of the way we manage the work process, up to a quarter of our employees do nothing but fix the mistakes of co-workers. Continuing along this path will be perilous for our country."

Continuous improvement requires a radical change in the way organizations go about their business. And it is precisely in periods of change that they most need leadership in order to create new values and new breakthroughs. Leaders of quality companies recognize that a strategy of continuous improvement requires decision making at every level of the organization, and they focus on creating an environment in which every employee has the power and support to contribute to positive change.

8 *Quality Is Not Enough*

In just a little more than a decade, many U.S. companies have made tremendous progress both in improving the quality of their products and services and in creating more participative workplaces. The American quality movement has been a true revolution: perhaps never in the history of American business has a philosophical change of this magnitude swept across the land so swiftly.

In typical American fashion each company has created a unique version of quality improvement, piecing together its own quality quilt from all available programs, theories, and strategies so that no one is exactly like any other.

Already there are signs that American quality improvement efforts are evolving away from attempts to mimic the Japanese, and in many companies "quality" now encompasses more than simply improving the quality of products and services. Du Pont no longer has a vice president of quality, but it does have a vice president of continuous improvement. At Fluor Daniel, the title is vice president for performance improvement. At IBM they've added the words "market-driven" to describe the company's quality-improvement efforts. AMP and Milliken are still pursuing "excellence"—the early 1980s Tom Peters' word that serves as the umbrella for many company efforts. And new contenders—like Six Sigma, Motorola's sexy slogan for quality improvement—are catching on. Our current favorite is TQP (for those who need an acronym): Total Quality Performance, coined by Hyman Katz at the Pall Corporation on Long Island.

There are two major reasons for the movement away from a strictly quality focus. One is the growing realization that simply working on improving products and services is not, alone, enough to build sustainable competitive advantage. Despite their great comebacks in the 1980s, for example, Ford and Caterpillar entered the 1990s still struggling financially. Florida Power & Light has been dismantling much of the "quality bureaucracy" that it created on the road to the Deming Prize.

The second reason is the realization that people are the key to making continuous improvement work. While Japan's manufacturing techniques are transplantable, its approaches to people are not. The apparent success of NUMMI notwithstanding, American and Japanese workers have such radically different cultural orientations that merely grafting Japanese human resources techniques onto an American organization—without modification—cannot possibly work over the long term.

James Fallows, the Washington editor of *The Atlantic Monthly,* who lived in Japan for several years, has the best definition of the differences we've seen:

Japan gets the most out of ordinary people by organizing them to adapt and succeed. America, by getting out of their way so that they can adjust individually, allows them to succeed. It is not that Japan has no individualists and America no organizations, but the thrust of the two societies is different. Japan has distorted its economy to keep its job structure and social values as steady as possible. . . . America's strength is the opposite: it opens its doors and brings the world's disorder in. It tolerates social change that would tear most other societies apart. This openness encourages Americans to adapt as individuals rather than as a group.[1]

These fundamental cultural differences make transplanting Japanese approaches to worker motivation and change a difficult proposition indeed.

The progressive quality companies that have begun expanding their efforts beyond traditional quality improvement understand what we consider to be a basic concept: quality is just the beginning. It is the first order of business. You can't come to the table without it. But quality is not enough.

THE BALDRIGE EFFECT

Because the Baldrige Award has in a few short years been accepted as a national arbiter of quality, it may be useful to examine the award for the way in which it reflects the strengths and limitations of quality improvement, and how it defines what quality is and is not.

The Baldrige Award campaign has been spectacularly successful in raising awareness of the benefits of quality improvement in American industry. One of the award's biggest boosters is Robert Galvin, the former chairman of Motorola, who presided over his company during a transformation that made it the first company-wide Fortune 500 company to win the Baldrige Award. He believes that the award should be a national policy; that every company should be considered a candidate. (Motorola has required all of its suppliers to apply, or to say when they will apply, for the award.)

Galvin calculates that if every company in America applied—made the investment that is required to apply—the Gross National Product would grow by a minimum of one half of one percent. Since American business eschews anything that looks like a national industrial policy, and voluntary compliance will probably not achieve Galvin's goal, he is not likely to get his wish. But it's a provocative calculation.

As a tool for assessing the quality improvement processes of a company, the Baldrige criteria are rigorous and demanding. They do not support or foster the status quo: they demand change. However, *the Baldrige Award program is a limited assessment of processes subjectively measured against a fixed set of general criteria by an average of five examiners (quality experts) from industry and academia and a comparable number of judges, who use a disci-plined but time-limited process to read and analyze an application and then verify the application's content through on-site visitations.* The threshold for earning a Baldrige site visit is around 750 points out of a possible 1,000—about a "C" in high school. The judges' decision does not have to be unanimous; a simple majority will suffice.

When Cadillac became the first broad-based consumer product to win the award, the ensuing controversy pointed up a gap in the understanding of the Baldrige Award criteria that exists among the general public as well as in the informed quality community. After the award was announced, everyone who didn't own a Cadillac; had a relative who had a bad experience with a Cadillac; didn't like Roger Smith (the for-mer chairman and CEO of General Motors, who was por-trayed in an unflattering manner in a popular, inaccurate, but amusing pseudo-documentary); didn't know (or care) about the internal process improvements that Cadillac had imple-mented; wasn't aware of the fact that Cadillac first applied for the award in 1989—as did Ford (both got site visits); didn't know that Cadillac not only made improvements based on their 1989 experience but showed great courage in applying again (running the real risk of being labeled a two-time loser)—said: "What? Cadillac won a quality award? You've got to be kidding!"

The detractors had somehow lost sight of the fact that the Baldrige Award is not a Consumer Union Report or a Good Housekeeping Seal of Approval. It is not a J. D. Powers report or consumer poll. It is not a Gallup Survey or *Fortune* corpo-rate-reputation (most-admired company) survey. It is not a market share barometer.

We don't want to get letters from people who bought Cadil-lacs in the early and mid-1980s, but—on the basis of the Baldrige criteria—Cadillac won fair and square. (To some ex-tent, the Baldrige judgment has been confirmed by other mea-sures. Cadillac has finished first among domestic cars in customer-satisfaction surveys by J. D. Powers for three consec-utive years and climbed to fifth from fourteenth among foreign and domestic cars. GM surveys show that defects in Eldorados and Sevilles have plunged 44 percent since 1986.)

LIMITATIONS OF THE BALDRIGE AWARD

Because the Baldrige Award is so visible, and because it provides a useful standard for assessing quality, hundreds of American companies have adopted the Baldrige criteria (see Appendix A) as the new foundation of their quality improvement efforts. This, as we've mentioned earlier, is a mixed blessing. To the extent that the standards are a catalyst, or starting point, for companies to focus on improving everything they do (including those things not specifically addressed), the criteria are an invaluable tool. To the extent that they divert attention from other—equally critical—management issues, they may be a liability.

The Baldrige criteria were never intended to be a measure of the overall competitive health of a company. They do not, for example, address such areas as financial performance, innovation, long-term planning, or environmental issues—all vital to success in the 1990s.

1. *Financial Performance.* Ironically, under the present criteria it's possible for a money-losing company to win the Award. But profitability is, has always been, and will always be the number-one priority of any company. Quality is arguably the best way to get there and is undeniably the only way to stay there, but one should not confuse the means with the end. Until a firm connection between continuous improvement and the bottom line is made, measured, and regularly reported to senior management, the people in the executive suite are not going to take quality seriously.

The commonly accepted wisdom is that the cost of poor quality averages 25 cents or more of each sales dollar. Virtually all quality improvement programs can document, to some degree, cost savings and cost reductions, but they are all hard-pressed to show a connection to profitability. There is a whole science of quality cost management (poor quality costs) that includes prevention and appraisal cost and measures internal and external error cost, but these activities are not driven by the chief financial officer's office; they are tools of the quality professionals.

We know of no company that has *fully* integrated its financial performance activities with its quality improvement programs. Baldrige winner Milliken might have, but Milliken is privately held and isn't talking. There have been some efforts in this area, but there has been no widespread endorsement or embracing of quality improvement by Wall Street or by the finance/management side of business. Quite simply, the relationship of quality improvement to financial performance has not been adequately documented in the United States.

2. *Innovation*. Technology has forced the pace of change and sharply cut the effective lifetimes of all kinds of products and services. The American problem is not innovation per se (from the airplane to PCs, overnight mail to fast food, we've always been great at inventing things), but the speed with which new or improved products are brought to market.

The Council on Competitiveness, a Washington-based organization of industry, labor, and higher education heavyweights, started by Hewlett-Packard CEO John Young and now chaired by George Fisher, chairman and CEO of Motorola, recognized the problem in a report titled *Picking Up the Pace: The Commercial Challenge to American Innovation*.

Written primarily by the Council's vice president, Dan Burton, the report focuses on the fact that American companies are being battered by companies from countries without large scientific bases who make up for their research shortcomings by concentrating their resources on rapid commercialization of new ideas.

One of the report's key findings: "Many of America's problems stem from not rapidly moving new innovations into the marketplace. . . ." The report says:

> When the United States so thoroughly dominated the world economy, the speedy translation of new ideas into practical products and processes was not a crucial factor in commercial success. International competition has changed that situation. For technology-based industry, a failure to focus on the rapid application of new ideas can be devastating.[2]

Many of the best American corporations—Motorola, Milliken, IBM, General Electric—have made cycle time reduction part of their quality improvement efforts. Others need to follow suit.

3. *Environment/Waste Management*. Waste management is classic quality control. Serious corporate environmentalism, like quality, begins with a commitment from senior management to consistently support improvement efforts, even when the choices are difficult. It requires training and empowerment to focus employee attitudes on raising the operating standards of the company. It requires accurate measurement systems for assessing how well the corporation is meeting the needs of its stakeholders, including—in the case of environmentalism—not merely owners, employees, and customers, but society at large.

Like the best quality processes, a strong environmental management system provides a permanent intellectual mechanism for transforming the goal of sustainable development into a business reality.

The Office of Technology Assessment estimates that U.S. manufacturing wastes can be halved using existing technologies. R&D could produce another 25 percent reduction. That translates into better quality and a lot of money saved. 3M's Pollution Prevention Pays program has saved more than $500 million since it was launched in 1975.

Companies have another, perhaps even more important, reason for being interested in better environmental practices. Today's kids—tomorrow's adult consumers—are the most environmentally conscious generation in history. Their preference—demand—for "environmentally friendly" products (regardless of their "quality") will almost certainly be the major differentiator in the years ahead.

4. *Policy Deployment/Planning*. American companies have serious shortcomings in both long- and short-term planning. The demand from the financial community for immediate profits makes long-term planning difficult if not impossible. Plans are made and quickly abandoned when they fail to show instant results.

American companies are also weak in the area of making plans operational rather than simply "what if" exercises. In this regard the Japanese provide a useful model. They call their approach to operational planning *hoshin kanri,* which literally means "gleaming metal" or "pointing direction." In the West, this approach is known as policy deployment. To begin, top management creates a vision of the company roughly five years in the future (in Japan it is ten, twenty, even fifty years out) which incorporates specific annual improvements in quality, cost, and delivery. This vision is "deployed" throughout the organization through specific detailed action plans developed at each management level, thus assuring "buy-in" at all levels. The action plans at one level of the company are linked directly to the objectives of the level above. Thus, the means to achieve a particular goal at one level become the end for the level below.

Policy deployment is a disciplined approach to continuous improvement that focuses everyone in the organization on the four or five key goals that top management wants to accomplish each year. This is materially different from the kind of Strategic Quality Planning covered by the Baldrige. Sooner or later, companies that are serious about continuous improvement will find their way to policy deployment.

The Baldrige Award is not a comprehensive business award; it is a quality practices award. It was never intended to rescue businesses or be the master plan for competitiveness; this extra responsibility has been thrust on it because of its enormous appeal to business and the absence of any other national criteria. It is necessary to keep in mind that, although quality is essential to competitiveness, there are other factors that cannot be ignored. The Baldrige criteria are not enough.

TQM: A CAUTIONARY TALE

Many American companies have adopted Total Quality Management, an Americanized version of Japanese company-wide quality control, as the foundation of their improvement efforts. Some have made great strides, but there are growing indications that TQM—like the Baldrige criteria—has its limitations as an all-embracing model for continuous improvement. In this regard, the saga of Florida Power & Light, the American company that has come closest to adopting the complete Japanese approach to company-wide quality control, is instructive.

In 1983 Marshall McDonald, then FPL's chairman, met Shoichiro Kobayashi, president of Kansai Electric Power Company, which supplies power to central Japan and is one of the largest utilities in the world, at the 1983 U.S.-Japan Electric Power Companies High Level Meeting. Kobayashi told McDonald about Kansai's quality-improvement efforts and invited him—and other FPL executives—to come have a look. Thus was born a close relationship between the companies.

After Kansai became the first Japanese service company to win the Deming Prize in 1984, McDonald and his successor as FPL chief executive, John Hudiburg, asked Kobayashi to help them convince the Union of Japanese Scientists and Engineers (JUSE), the organization that directs the Deming Prize, to provide JUSE counselors to FPL. This created something of a dilemma since no American company had asked JUSE for help before, and the counselors weren't convinced that FPL was sincere. Finally they agreed to do so on a trial basis.

The quality improvement process that evolved from the FPL-JUSE collaboration has three major components, all supported by extensive education and training programs:

Policy Deployment, a "top down" effort for achieving customer satisfaction by focusing and deploying resources on a few high-priority issues, mainly involving customers, reliability, and employee safety; *Quality in Daily Work (QIDW),* a decentralized system for standardizing initial improvements, replicating them in other locations, or monitoring work process at the local level; and *Quality Improvement Teams,* introduced to allow employees to use their creativity in solving problems and to be heard by management.

Over the next six years, FPL enjoyed spectacular results, earning a reputation for having the best quality-improvement process in the nation. In 1989 it became the first non-Japanese company to win Japan's Deming Prize, the highest award for outstanding achievement in quality management, after a rigorous, year-long application effort, including site visits from JUSE quality auditors.

To the outside world, FPL looked like the fount of all knowledge in the quality improvement area. But, unknown to even the most sophisticated observers of the quality revolution, the passionate emphasis on TQM was quietly tearing the company apart, demoralizing employees, and preventing a lot of important work from being done.

In the spring of 1990, FPL Group chairman and CEO James L. Broadhead met with more than 500 randomly selected employees in small groups to hear their opinions and concerns. What concerned them most was the fear that the company's quality-improvement process had become a tyrannical bureaucracy.

While acknowledging that quality and customer satisfaction are important and that they had learned valuable analytical tools from quality improvement training, the majority of employees Broadhead talked to said they thought the mechanics of QIP had been overemphasized.

In a memo circulated in May, Broadhead said: "They [employees] felt that we place too great an emphasis on indicators, charts, graphs, reports, and meetings in which documents are presented and indicators reviewed. These employees believe that undue emphasis on process deprives them of time that could be better spent serving customers and participating in community affairs, and has resulted in their having to work extraordinarily hard merely to fulfill the basic requirements of their jobs. Among other things, they recommended reducing the number of indicators tracked, reports prepared and meetings held, and eliminating formal or informal quotas for IAMs and 'Bright Ideas.'

"I was most troubled, however, by the frequently stated opinion that preoccupation with process had resulted in our losing sight of one of the major tenets of quality improvement, namely, respect for employees. Many employees mentioned that there is too little personal responsibility for results, and that there is less recognition for making good business decisions than for following the QI process. They said their views on improving the process were never solicited and were not well received when voluntarily contributed."

Broadhead wasted no time in responding. In June he circulated another memo in which he essentially undid what his predecessor, Marshall McDonald, had spent many years doing.

"With the Deming examination behind us, it is time to go beyond our developmental emphasis on procedures and to accentuate those activities that have a more direct impact on the achievement of excellence. Employees must have the freedom to innovate, to solve problems, to perform their jobs, without the fear that they will be criticized for not following one particular format or methodology." Broadhead then announced seven specific steps designed to reduce the quality bureaucracy.

1. The Quality Improvement Department, the Quality Improvement Promotion Group, and Quality Support Services were eliminated and their personnel reassigned to other positions.

2. Three levels of reviews were eliminated.

3. Executive visits were eliminated. Said Broadhead: "There is little value in having an executive who is not responsible for a department and who is unfamiliar with its operation take the time of many individuals to check indicators and monitor conformity to a rigid process."

4. All departments and divisions were directed to review indicators, teams, and reports with the goal of streamlining and simplifying the quality process.

5. Quotas for quality teams, community involvement activities, IAMs, and Bright Ideas were eliminated. "These quotas engender neither quality nor productivity, and they are inconsistent with respect for people."

6. The QI Story Seven-Step Process is no longer mandatory for problem solving. "The emphasis will be on continuous improvement and finding answers that benefit the company and its customers, not on using a prescribed methodology."

7. FPL's training program, which has been overwhelmingly QIP related, is being redesigned to provide more training in supervisory skills and customer sensitivity concepts, as well as quality improvement techniques. Quality improvement courses that had been five-day courses are becoming two- or three-day courses.

"Some will say that these acts constitute an abandonment of our quality program," Broadhead admitted. "Nothing could be further from the truth. . . . We have an outstanding company and I'm confident that we will become even better."

History will of course judge whether or not Broadhead

threw the baby out with the bathwater. But for those companies pinning their hopes on TQM, FPL's retrenchment is a troubling event indeed.

What Is Enough?

If the Baldrige criteria are not enough to get a company into top competitive shape, what is?

Phil Crosby's landmark book, *Quality Is Free,* published in 1979, is all about quality. It was the most influential book in launching the American quality revolution, and it doesn't mention customer satisfaction.

Tom Peters' book, *In Search of Excellence,* published in 1982, is all about customer satisfaction. It did for the customer satisfaction movement what Crosby's book did for quality. Yet, equally striking, it does not mention quality.

Each man is credited, properly, with starting a vital revolution of thought and action in America. However, neither of them identified the third essential element that is revolutionizing the thinking and action of world-class quality companies today. That element is innovation.

The quality revolution has its roots in manufacturing, on the factory floor. It gave business Technical Quality—essentially an internal focus on product quality that relies on quality tools and technology. The customer is persuaded or convinced to take the product or service.

The service industry gave business Functional Quality—essentially externally focused processes that rely more on people and human judgments than quality tools and technology.

What happened in the 1980s is that manufacturing and service industries began to learn from each other and to swap strategies. Manufacturing companies discovered the customer, and service industries discovered the benefits of technical process controls.

Happily, but not rapidly, some manufacturing and some service companies have now begun to incorporate some of the elements in the third stage of quality that we call Competitive Quality. The focus of Competitive Quality is on the total market, not just the product or existing customer base.

What remains is level four: Forward Quality. This concept is beginning to emerge, but we have as yet seen no definition of it. For us, Forward Quality is synonymous with innovation. Like innovation, it is focused on new markets, new worlds, and the broadening of product and service offerings. The key to customer retention and recruitment is building a relationship of trust.

INCREMENTAL STAGES OF CONTINUOUS IMPROVEMENT

Technical Quality

Focus:	internal products or processes
Measure:	doing things right
Driver:	cost
Relies on:	quality tools, process, and technology
Customer perspective:	persuade them

Functional Quality

Focus:	external customers
Measure:	customer satisfaction
Driver:	process
Relies on:	people and judgment
Customer perspective:	satisfy them

Competitive Quality

Focus:	total market
Measure:	market share
Driver:	value
Relies on:	time and flexibility
Customer perspective:	attract them

Forward Quality

Focus:	new markets
Measure:	new product/service offerings
Driver:	innovation
Relies on:	long-term planning, intuition
Customer perspective:	build trust

At this time, there are only a handful of companies that are starting to discover that their quality practices and customer strategies, now securely in place, have driven them to the next level of the quality revolution—innovation. Strategies that are an outgrowth of the improvement process are taking on a life of their own, and innovations, both in products and processes, are the consequence.

WHAT BALDRIGE APPLICANTS DON'T KNOW ABOUT QUALITY

Most American companies—even those that have applied for the award—really don't know how bad their quality performance is. While preparing this book, we surveyed forty Baldrige examiners drawn at random from the list of 178 provided to us by the American Society for Quality Control and asked them—among other things—what were the biggest surprises or weaknesses they had noted in the applications they had reviewed. They identified the weaknesses as:

> Failure to match actions to words about leadership.
> (Baldrige Examination Category 1.0: Leadership. 100 points)

Although leadership was overall one of the stronger sections of most applications, 36 percent of the examiners identified major weaknesses in this category. These weaknesses were not immediately evident (Americans are good with words, and Baldrige applications are no exception). The examiners did not quarrel with the wordsmithing as much as they did with the inconsistencies in the remainder of the application: the actions detailed in the other categories did not match the words in Category 1.*

This isn't the only place the gap between words and action has been identified. In ASQC's 1990 annual Gallup Survey (the only national survey that has been measuring the quality

---

*See Appendix A.

attitudes and practices of American business, adult consumers, and employees annually since 1985), employees were asked two related questions about policy objectives within their companies: (1) To what extent does their company say something is important? (2) To what extent does their company act on what they say is important?

For example, when asked to rate their companies on a 10-point scale, more than half (55 percent) reported that their company says it is extremely important (10) that customers are shown that the company is committed to quality. Yet only 36 percent gave their companies a 10 for follow-through.[3]

The Baldrige examiners we surveyed also told us that "tough goals are not being set by CEOs." In addition, they cited the most prevalent action taken by a CEO after voicing commitment to quality was to turn over the responsibility to a division president, a vice president, or a steering committee, without further substantive, personal involvement.

Failure to understand benchmarking.
(Category 2.0: Information and Analysis. 70 points)

Sixty percent of examiners identified major weaknesses in the Information and Analysis category. This is the category that is essentially equated with benchmarking.

With all of the available knowledge and publicity on benchmarking, popularized by Xerox, this shortcoming in the Baldrige applications may have been the biggest surprise. The concept was either totally misunderstood or was thought to apply to industry comparisons only: Who in my industry does what the best? Few of the total number of 203 applicants (from 1988–90), beyond the thirty-five companies that received a site visit, grasped the full dimensions and strategic value of benchmarking.

Several examiners noted that the benchmarking concept was stronger in manufacturing companies than in service companies. In fact, service companies in general did not have a strong sense of an external standard; this, some examiners suggested, was due to the general lack of foreign competition in the service markets.

Failure to involve employees.
(Category 4.0: Human Resource Utilization. 150 points)

Approximately half the examiners in our survey (48 percent) identified major weaknesses in the Human Resource Utilization category. The most discouraging discovery: most formal human resource departments do not support (or are not a part of) quality objectives and training.

One imagines that all employees at all Baldrige winners are involved in quality improvement all the time. Nothing could be further from the truth, with the possible exception of the small-business winners, where the number of employees and size of the company make this ideal objective more feasible.

What is true of the larger Baldrige-winner companies is that more employees are involved more of the time than in non-Baldrige companies. According to the 1990 ASQC/Gallup Survey, the national average is 66 percent participation in companies that have a quality improvement program; indications are that the Baldrige winners have a 10 to 15 percent greater involvement.[4] A goal of 75 to 80 percent participation is well within striking distance of those companies striving to be "Baldrige eligible," but it is greatly outdistanced by Japanese competitors, where the evidence is that many manufacturing industries have achieved total involvement.

QUALITY AWARDS: WHAT'S IN A NAME?

Psychiatrists and psychoanalysts could have a field day with the conscious (and unconscious) reasons for the choices made by the Japanese and Americans in naming their nation's top quality award. For starters, the Japanese choice was no doubt deliberate and well thought out. In America it was impulsive, inspired by the untimely death of Secretary of Commerce Malcolm Baldrige, whose department was designated to administer the award program.

The choice of W. Edwards Deming, a living legend, was a brilliant—and unwittingly mischievous—marketing choice for the Japanese. Ironically, it stands in dramatic contrast to a

memorial for an obscure cabinet official in the Reagan Administration who is now remembered as a Cowboy Hall of Famer
who met his death in a rodeo accident.

For those who try to do the right things right the first time,
there is more than a little irony in the spelling of Baldrige's
name. Malcolm used to spell his name with an extra "d":
Baldridge. When he learned through a family discussion that
the name originally had only one "d" and that it had been
Americanized to Baldridge, he reverted to the original spelling.
As a consequence, countless people today, invoking his name
in the name of quality, misspell it. The matter is further con-
fused by the fact that Malcolm's brother, a trustee of the Foundation for the Malcolm Baldrige National Quality Award,
spells his name with the extra "d."

Still another irony is that Baldrige had been a young lieuten-
ant in the 27th Infantry Division in Okinawa during the war
and was one of the first Americans to land in Japan in the first
week after the surrender. Although he normally kept his opinions private, he was—according to Theodore White—the
most prominent member of the Reagan Administration to
believe that the Japanese advantage was deliberate unfair trade
practices, not quality.

The final irony is that the namesake of the Deming award
never ran a company or made it to upper management. Baldrige, by contrast, served as chairman and chief executive
officer of Scovill, Inc., in Waterbury, Connecticut. He joined
Scovill in 1962 and he is credited with leading its transformation from a financially troubled brass mill to a highly diversified
manufacturer of consumer, housing, and industrial goods. Few
Americans, however, know anything about his career before
his arrival in Washington.

Ironies aside, the prize names may be more appropriate than
they seem at first blush. It is somehow fitting that the Japanese,
with their formality and serious approach to quality, have
chosen to revere a humorless, all-business guru of quality who
by many accounts is something of a curmudgeon. Americans,
on the other hand, with their penchant for John Wayne-style
heroics, have named their prize for a New Englander who in
spite of his management experiences was really a cowboy who
died with his boots on.

9 *The Innovators*

WHAT MAKES a company an innovator? Although a commonly accepted definition is illusive, we believe innovative companies have some, or all, of the following characteristics: they are the best, or nearly the best, in their industry; they are growing faster and more profitably than most of their competitors; they hire and retain the best people; they respond quickly to changing market conditions; they are not satisfied with the status quo; they continually upgrade facilities, processes, and skills once considered state-of-the-art.

In our study of dozens of American companies, we have identified a number of other specific practices that distinguish innovative competitors from their run-of-the-mill brethren.

INNOVATORS EMPOWER THEIR WORKERS

Empowerment is one of those trendy, popular-psychology words that somehow invite derision. That is unfortunate because it is a vital concept in building a quality organization. Empowerment means giving employees the authority and information they need to make wise business decisions and solve problems. This in turn enhances the working environment and leads to personal satisfaction. And a profound lesson of the quality movement is that worker satisfaction is inseparable

157

from customer satisfaction. A company whose employees are improperly trained, are kept in the dark about overall strategy, and have no authority to act—within reasonable parameters—on behalf of customers cannot be a quality company.

Empowerment often scares workers because people are fallible, and implicit in the authority to act is the possibility of failure. As Jan Carlzon, chairman of SAS, says: "If front-line employees are actually to make decisions that entail some risk, they must have a sense of security. Having knowledge and information is not enough if they believe a wrong decision may cause them problems or even the loss of their job. They must know that they are allowed to make mistakes. Only then will they dare to use fully their new authority."[1]

If empowerment scares line workers, it terrifies managers, who frequently see it as a lessening of their authority. Though misplaced, this fear is often a serious obstacle to success. As Dr. G. Clotaire Rapaille, president, Archetype Studies, puts it: "The paradox of empowerment is that in order to gain power, you must give some of it away. Good managers are those who recognize that empowerment is not a substitute for leadership or a diminution of their own authority. The more people are empowered, the more they need leaders who can set goals and define a vision of where the organization should be going."

Empowerment requires that management choose and communicate goals that every employee can rally around, and define the strategies for accomplishing them. For Milliken & Co., that process began with a thorough re-examination of every facet of its organization.

In 1980 Milliken, a major textile manufacturer long recognized for quality products and its use of state-of-the-art technology, asked itself why some Japanese competitors achieved higher quality, less waste, greater productivity, and fewer customer complaints while using technology less advanced than its own. The reasons, company executives found, lay in management approaches and in personnel practices that, along with technology, drive improvements in quality and efficiency.

In 1981 senior management set in motion Milliken's Pursuit of Excellence (POE), a commitment to customer satisfaction that pervades all company levels at all locations.

The wisdom of a "customer-driven and quality-focused"

approach to manufacturing and nonmanufacturing activities is verified by its success. Since the early 1980s, productivity has increased 42 percent, and sales have risen significantly. As icing on the cake, Milliken was awarded the Malcolm Baldrige National Quality Award in 1989.

The 125-year-old privately owned company employs 14,300 workers, or what the company terms "associates," most at Milliken's forty-seven manufacturing facilities in the United States. The company has achieved a flat management structure in which associates, working primarily in self-managed teams, exercise considerable authority and autonomy. Production work teams, for example, can undertake training, schedule work, and establish individual performance objectives. Moreover, any of Milliken's associates can halt a production process if that person detects a quality or safety problem.

The approach has worked so well that Milliken has reduced the number of management positions by nearly 700 since 1981, freeing a large portion of the work force for assignment as process improvement specialists. There has been a 77 percent increase in the ratio of production to management associates.

The Milliken philosophy is neatly summed up by Newt Hardie, vice president—quality: "Our role as leaders is not to catch people doing things wrong but to create an environment in which people can become heroes."

Innovators Are Market-Driven

The profound leadership lesson of the 1980s is that the needs and expectations of customers are not fixed; they are constantly changing. World-class companies must know what products and services their customers want to buy now.

These realities are not lost on IBM chairman John Akers. Since he took over the helm of Big Blue in 1985, the ex–fighter pilot has systematically been restructuring the venerable company in an attempt to restore its pre-eminence as a technology and product leader and make it more market-driven.

"We've always been a conservative organization, partly by habit and partly as a result of the success we've had," Akers says. "It quickly became clear to me that while our customers still had a deep reservoir of trust and confidence in IBM, they thought we had become too complex, too difficult to do business with; our product cycles were too long, and we weren't telling them enough about our product directions."

By any objective measure, IBM is not doing all that badly. America's most valuable company (market value: $69 billion) finished the 1980s pretty much where it started—number one in the computer industry worldwide. With sales five times those of its nearest rival, IBM has the broadest product range and the biggest sales force. It spends more on R&D each year than any four of its competitors.

From 1964, when it introduced the System/360, its first family of compatible computers, until the early 1980s, IBM was the unchallenged leader in the business. Although it was a latecomer to the PC market, the IBM marketing magic rang up 6 million sales between 1981 and 1986. When the company introduced the PS/2 in 1987, the worldwide installation base of IBM and IBM-compatible PCs was 15 million. Ironically, it was precisely this "democratization" of computing power that created problems for the company.

"A funny thing happened to us on the way to the bank," says Stephen B. Schwartz, senior vice president—market-driven quality. "Our very success kicked up a storm of change in the industry. For the first time, ordinary people—people without degrees in computer science—were interacting directly with a computer. They were looking at computers from a new perspective. They wanted them to be easier to use. They wanted them to operate in integrated networks. They wanted more application solutions to their specific business requirements. They wanted computers to exchange information so that employees could have access to information they needed in their jobs and could communicate with one another. In too many cases, we found out that IBM systems were not meeting these new demands."

It quickly became obvious to Akers, as well as outsiders, that IBM needed to rethink the way it did business. The company's market share has fallen with each succeeding generation of computer technology. While it holds half of the world market in mainframes, which were state-of-the-art in the 1960s, it holds only 15 percent of the market for smaller, more flexible machines of the minicomputer/work station variety, and slightly more than 10 percent of the personal computer market. While its markets have grown by 15 percent a year since 1985, IBM's sales have averaged less than 6 percent growth during that period.

In November 1986 Akers invited six major IBM customers to sit down with eighteen of the company's senior executives at headquarters in Purchase, New York, to talk about the company's product, service, and software directions for the next decade. It was the first time in the tradition-bound company's seventy-two-year history that customers had participated in one of IBM's regular top-level strategy meetings. The IBMers got an earful.

"We learned a lot of things," Akers says. "We learned that we weren't as communicative as we really needed to be. It quickly became clear that all of our competitors in the industry were sharing their product plans and future directions much more aggressively and eagerly with our customers than we were. We were spending more than $5 billion a year in our R&D operations to develop better products for our customers, but we really weren't talking about that with them much. Therefore they had a difficult time in planning because they didn't have a clear view as to what was coming from IBM, and we weren't using their perspective as well as we should in bending and shaping our development efforts. That was the major activity we changed as a result of those discussions."

Akers immediately set out to eliminate barriers to direct customer contact. In his first four years, he removed two layers of management and reduced the U.S. work force by 37,000 people—including 7,000 management positions—without compromising the company's long-standing full-employment policy. About 20 percent of the company's personnel were shifted into the marketing and support organization, where they would be more accessible to customers.

The company has made herculean efforts to make itself easier for customers to do business with. Until recently, for example, IBM's sales force was organized by product and by country. That made it difficult to put together systems that combined IBM products from different countries or product groups. Now IBM is organizing its sales force by customer, or, for smaller companies, by industry. The company has spent millions on training its salesmen on the application of its software on an industry-by-industry basis. It is up to the sales representative for each company, or industry, to get what his customers need from the rest of the organization—no matter where it is made.

Until 1989 multinational companies—which account for a quarter of sales—had to deal separately with local IBM offices in each country where they did business. Today they have the option of one-stop shopping through a global marketing program. More than four-fifths of them leaped at the chance.

Over the past four years the company has established strategic alliances with thousands of business partners in computer services and application development to improve customer support and expand customer solutions. It has added thousands of people to its own corps of programmers to develop in-house solution software offerings. Maintenance offerings have been improved, terms and conditions have been simplified, contract paperwork cut, and billing has been streamlined. A tired product line has been revitalized.

"Most of all, we've directed our entire strategy outward, focusing on the customer's goals and needs, the customer's priorities, the customer's productivity, competitiveness, and profits," says Stephen Schwartz. "In other words we've become a market-driven company with the goal of defect-free quality in everything we do."

Encouraged by this success and by improvements realized by broad approaches to quality in different parts of the corporation, IBM officially launched its most intensive and far-reaching continuous-improvement process in history in January 1990. Called Market-Driven Quality (MDQ), the program involves five major initiatives:

- Define the needs of the market
- Eliminate defects
- Reduce total cycle time
- Increase employee participation
- Measure progress

Senior executives have been named "owners" of the initiatives; systems for analyzing the flow of business and assessing the company's performance against the competition (as well as world-class companies in other industries) have been implemented; and the Malcolm Baldrige National Quality Award has been adopted as the mechanism by which IBM will measure itself worldwide.

Akers has set some very tough goals for the MDQ campaign. By the time he is scheduled to retire in 1994, he expects IBM's worldwide organization to cut product-development cycle time by half and reduce defects by a staggering factor of 100. As a central initiative, IBM has adopted Motorola's Six Sigma approach to eliminating defects, which translates into 3.4 defects per million. In January 1990 the company was running at about three sigma or 66,800 defects per million—about average for all U.S. manufacturing.

"A virtually defect-free operation sounds impossible but it's not," says Stephen Schwartz. "Many Japanese companies and a few American companies like Motorola are well on their way to being there. We intend to do it through scrupulous gathering of data, applying measurements, identifying root causes of defects, and then eliminating them in a systematic way."

Cutting product-development cycle time is MDQ's other primary initiative. In a business where a product is now considered mature after two years and ancient after five, the typical four-to-five-year development cycle for bringing a midrange computer to market is no longer acceptable. That means speeding up design, development, manufacture, ordering, shipping, and billing and, most importantly, staying completely abreast of customer requirements. Much emphasis is being placed on intelligence-gathering or "market information capture," as the company calls it. The company is combining its many market research databases into one, so that complete and consistent information can be disseminated to IBMers around the world.

How IBM Cut Cycle Time and Improved Quality

When IBM launched its market-driven quality process, it found it had a world-class model for both defect- and cycle-time reduction in its own Application Business System's division in Rochester, Minnesota, winner of the 1990 Baldrige Award. IBM Rochester makes the company's highly successful AS/400 intermediate computer systems. Development of the AS/400 began in 1986, and the replacement for IBM's old S/36 and S/38 machines reached market in 1988—less than half the time it had taken to bring its predecessors to market.

In a break with tradition, IBM Rochester involved customers in the process from the beginning, creating customer advisory councils with whom it shared its plans for the new machines. One early suggestion that was adopted was to make it easier for buyers to transfer programs and data from their old machines to the new computers. As a result, IBM agreed to share software codes with other manufacturers of equipment being used by customers. By the time the AS/400 was introduced, potential buyers had tested 1,700 of the machines, and IBM made further refinements based on their suggestions.

Using cross-functional teams that merged software and hardware design with manufacturing, IBM Rochester employed a variety of innovations to reduce cycle time. For example, engineers developed a machine that allowed them to simulate the results of various design possibilities until they achieved a virtually defect-free design. That process alone saved ten months.

On the software side, IBM Rochester applied a technique it calls the milestone process in which development of the 7 million lines of software code used in the AS/400—by far the largest single release in IBM history—was broken down into small modules and spread across dedicated software development groups. The modules were merged at each checkpoint and functionally tested, dramatically reducing cycle time and reducing error.

Early involvement between manufacturing and design teams led to simplification of manufacturing and greatly reduced costs. For example, the AS/400 has 4,000 parts; the old S/38 had 10,000 parts.

Knowing that programming would be the key to selling the new computer, the company brought independent software companies into the planning in early 1987. When the AS/400 was introduced simultaneously worldwide, there were more than 1,000 software applications packages available in twelve languages, including French, Japanese, and Chinese. IBM has called the introduction of the AS/400 the most successful product launch in its history.

Even after the system is shipped, IBM maintains the customer link. After ninety days, a "customer partner" call is made to check on whether there are any problems with the new installation. The company frequently uses IBM retirees, working part-time, to make many of the calls because of their familiarity with the company and its product line. Customer problems are referred to the local servicing group for action, and then a thirty-day follow-up ensures that the problem has been solved.

"Innovation is essential to reducing cycle time, and innovation takes many forms—technology, solutions, delivery, and support among them," says Stephen Schwartz, who was general manager of IBM Rochester during the development of the AS/400. "Innovation is delivering a total system package to a customer so all that is necessary, literally, is to uncrate the system, plug it in, and go to work."

INNOVATORS SEE THE WORLD DIFFERENTLY

Procter & Gamble, the name behind 165 household brands, last year had about $24 billion in sales in 140 countries. That's a lot of Crest toothpaste, Head & Shoulders shampoo, Vicks cold remedy, Ivory soap, and more than 80 other products that can be found in most homes. But the interesting statistic is that 40 percent of those sales were from abroad. For the Cincinnati-based consumer product innovator, that represents a big change from just ten years ago, when foreign sales represented only 15 percent of its business.

What accounts for this success? Edwin Artzt, chairman and CEO of P&G, told UCLA students at a recent recruiting seminar that it all boils down to "challenging traditional thinking." The first requirement for global success is breakthrough technology, which enables P&G to make products that deliver superior performance and value to all consumers. The second requirement is to tailor the product to fit the needs of consumers in different parts of the world; as Artzt says, "It requires that we know the habits, perfume preferences, physical characteristics of hair and skin."[2]

There are some things that P&G has found are basic to all consumer needs—the desire for more attractive complexions, drier babies, and cavity-free teeth. But important cultural differences in habits require product diversification.

Artzt cites two examples: (1) babies in the Middle East tend to dehydrate because of the hot weather and have lower urine output than babies in most other parts of the world, so mothers are more conscious of diapers that are too bulky or too tight fitting, (2) hair characteristics are different in Asia from those in the United States, so different levels of conditioning are needed in the two-in-one shampoo and conditioner products.

Not only must products be different, but marketing strategies must match customer expectations. Commercials for Tide in Japan had to stress the compact packaging, because the average family lives in a 500-square-foot apartment, but in the United States, where space is not a problem and washing machines are big, marketing had to focus on convenience aspects while still emphasizing performance.

Understanding the washing habits in Europe led to a major P&G product innovation—compact detergent called a granulette. Most European consumers use a two-step washing process—presoaking and washing. Two separate doses of detergent are put in different dispensing drawers built into the machine. P&G's new product eliminates the need for the dispensing drawers. The compact detergent goes right in with the clothes with no further fuss. It is premeasured, one step, and environmentally friendly—a special concern of all consumers in Europe, especially in Germany.

Artzt's vision for P&G: $50 billion in worldwide sales and earnings of $3 billion annually within the decade. In 1990 he told analysts at his first meeting with them as the new CEO that his strategy for achieving his vision was built on six factors:

- Globalization
- Technology-driven product development
- Strategic use of acquisitions and alliances

- Relentless pursuit of worldwide systems change to improve quality
- Proactive environmental program
- Organizational restructuring and programs designed to continue to push responsibility down closer to consumers and customers[3]

Coming from a company whose marketing strategy is "the key to marketing is superior product performance," Artzt's vision is good news for consumers—and bad news for competitors—the world over.

INNOVATORS TEST NEW IDEAS

No company has a quality legacy quite like AT&T's. The company was the pioneer of quality improvement; the inventor of much of today's quality technology, and the incubator for Shewhart, Deming, and Juran, who got their career starts at AT&T's Bell Labs and Hawthorne Works. So it should be no surprise that the company is an innovator today—involved in a perpetual search for new knowledge, new strategies, and opportunities to test new ideas and challenge old assumptions.

While most companies were struggling with quality and competitive pressures in the early 1980s, AT&T faced on January 1, 1984, a brave new world—the world of divestiture. Through all that turmoil, it was the company's roots in quality, we feel, that helped chart the new and still evolving diversified communications company. Much has changed since the days when the indestructible black rotary phones defined quality for most Americans, but AT&T's commitment to innovation has not.

Divestiture was a powerful crisis experience for AT&T. It forced the company to ask what to keep, what to change; what was working, what was not.

AT&T was among the first companies in America to look beyond the manufacturing process to see how quality improvement could be applied to service and administrative functions. Would what worked for products work for people? The answer was yes and then no.

Product and process improvement, statistical process control (SPC), and other quality technologies have an unambiguous language. They are easily understood. On the other hand, strategies for people quality, like Japan's quality circles, don't have a universal language or application. America's quality improvement strategies for people were not invented in America, much less at AT&T. And to no one's real surprise, American companies have not had much success with ideas and strategies they import.

In 1985 Ray Peterson, quality director of AT&T's Network Systems, and Marilyn Zuckerman, manager of quality planning, began an experiment that is starting to radically change the way Americans are looking at the human side of quality. They decided to see if they could find an American answer to what motivates people to improve and what inhibits that improvement.

It began with an analysis of the way companies manage. Their observations are simply stated but profound in their meaning:

OLD: Products > > > > > Process > > > > > People
NEW: People > > > > > Process > > > > > Products

They noted that most companies, including AT&T, focus exclusively on products or services and on the processes that have traditionally ensured the best possible results. People are then trained in those processes regardless of their compatibility. Essentially what AT&T started to ask was, What would happen if you reversed the course of events and started with people? Who are they? What makes them produce? What makes them tick? They then asked, What processes do they respond to most?

AT&T, like other companies of the 80s, was transplanting Japanese management ideas with no regard for cultural variabilities. The act of transplanting ideas was more important than seeing if those ideas bore fruit. Those who took the time to check saw little or no promise. What was wrong?

Zuckerman set the mission: "We wanted to understand how quality is perceived in America so that we could create a model that could work for Americans, both at home and in the workplace."

Their search led them to an outside consultant who seemed particularly well suited for the task. Dr. G. Clotaire Rapaille, a French-born psychologist and marketing expert, specializes in what he calls "archetype studies." Drawing upon Jungian and Gestalt theory, Rapaille's approach is to find the permanent structures—the mental codes or the emotional grammar—of people who are part of the same culture. These imprinted structures—the Jungian notion of the "collective unconscious"—are the archetype.

Beginning in February 1986 and continuing for ten months, AT&T and Rapaille conducted about a dozen archetype focus (imprinting) groups across the country with second-generation Americans representing a cross section of age, sex, race, and job function. Using discussion, games, and guided exercises, Rapaille helped people move beyond their opinions (on which most companies have based their understanding of people and the quality improvement process) to recall their first, most important, and most recent experience with quality. By analyzing the recurring structure (not content) in the participants' written descriptions of these experiences, Rapaille and the AT&T team led by Zuckerman were able to identify the American Quality Archetype™.

The results are startling and profound. The study's most surprising finding is that the first imprinting of quality that Americans have is strongly emotional and negative, triggered by not being able to measure up to someone's expectations. And the pattern repeated itself in the other experiences—reinforcing the imprinting.

No wonder that management's quality directives—"do it right the first time," "zero defects," "conformance to specifications," and "the customer is always right"—were creating cognitive dissonance in the workplace. No wonder that the imperative to seek perfection did not resonate with Americans at work.

The study also revealed that for Americans "quality" is

equated with "it works," while perfection connotes "the end," with no place to go, nothing left to do—a meaning that conflicts with the ideas of continuous improvement.

The study also introduced a new vocabulary for connecting the archetype findings with what Americans in the workplace needed to make quality happen. These words include: impossible dream, lawgiver, crisis, mentor, coach, celebration, and champion. Out go the traditional meanings. The impossible dream has a serious role in business (see sections on Disney and General Electric); mentors in the archetype definition don't help you on your way through the system but are there to identify with your emotions when things go wrong; coaches at work, like real coaches, help you practice your skills and they are there when it's your turn to bat again—they are not left in the corporate training rooms with the textbooks on process.

Using the results of the study, AT&T developed a transformation process—which is an emerging American model for continuous improvement. The model, tested at AT&T's Atlanta Works under the direction of Lew Hatala, quality manager, centers on a "champion" and his or her quest, struggle, failures, success, and ultimate celebration. The process begins with a "lawgiver" who communicates to the champion a crisis, an urgent need demanding action. The champion feels challenged and gets to work, but somewhere, early on, he encounters failure.

Enter the "mentor," who provides support in ways that help the champion understand the reality of the situation and release his guilt at having failed. By caring and helping renew a sense of purpose, the mentor helps the champion move past the negative feelings and try again. This time, however, he enlists the aid of the "coach," who supports and works with him, developing skills, insisting on practice, setting deadlines, and ultimately guiding the champion to victory.

The final role in the process is the "celebration," which recognizes the journey and achievements of the champion, reaffirms his worth, creates a positive memory, and energizes him to take on new challenges.

In addition to explaining why *Rocky* and *The Karate Kid* did so well at the box office, the quality archetype has many implications, not the least of which is that for Americans the emotional process of achieving quality is as important as the result. It also points to a need to sanction the free expression of emotions—good and bad—in the workplace. And in glorifying the roles of mentors and coaches, the quality model suggests that traditional managers should rethink their style and alter their behavior in order to become more effective leaders.

Innovators Make Customer Satisfaction an Obsession

One day back in 1984 Charlie Cawley, president and CEO of MBNA America, the hugely successful Newark, Delaware-based credit card company, happened to be walking through what was then called the customer relations department when he spotted a stack of letters from customers lying on a desk. He was aware through the usual reporting processes that there was a backlog in responding to customer correspondence but, like most senior managers, he was inclined to think of it as just another glitch at the departmental level that would soon be sorted out.

"I'm not sure why I did it because up to that time it was not the sort of thing I would normally do, but I sat down and started reading the letters," Cawley says. "After about the fifth letter, I picked them up and took them down to my office because I didn't want anyone to see how I was about to react. And I sat there until late in the evening reading them and getting more and more steamed. These were really simple things . . . 'I'm out of checks and this is the third time I've written you.' They weren't saying, 'you're terrible,' or anything like that; they were saying, 'we need more of your attention.'"

The next morning at eight o'clock, Cawley began the first of a series (the conference room held only 125 people) of five meetings that would include—before the end of the day—all 550 of the people who worked for the company at the time.

"I wasn't sure what I was going to say, so I just started reading the letters," Cawley says. "After five or six I started to get hot again—which is not a bad thing when you're trying to make a point. Before I read each one, I said, 'Pretend this is you.' And I could see people in the audience reacting like 'Jeez, this is awful.' "

Before the end of that first session Cawley had crystallized and articulated the philosophy that has since made MBNA America, by many measurements, the most successful credit card company in the business: "From this day forward, we are going to put the customer first."

MBNA was established in Delaware in 1982. Today it is the fourth-largest bank credit card company in the U.S. (trailing only long-established giants Citibank, Chase Manhattan, and First Chicago), with 3,600 people working round-the-clock, 365 days a year, to serve nearly 9 million customers wherever they happen to be at the time.

"There are really four key factors that have been critical to the success of the company," says Steve Boyden, senior vice president and head of the company's advertising efforts. "One is good timing—we were in the right place at the right time; second, an innovative marketing approach. We introduced the concept of endorsed credit card marketing with the American Dental Association in 1983, and today more than 1,700 professional associations, fraternal organizations, special interest groups, companies, and financial and educational institutions endorse our products. Third, we have grown in a controlled manner, putting quality service ahead of growth. And, most important of all, an absolute dedication to quality and customer satisfaction."

There is another factor in MBNA's success that Boyden doesn't mention because it might sound too self-serving but is immediately apparent to any objective visitor. That is what might be called "the Charlie factor." Mr. Cawley (or Charlie—never Charles) is a demanding, charming, and charismatic executive who likes singing in barbershop quartets and making customers happy. He loves his work, is emotional about it, and doesn't care who knows it. He has opinions on everything. Say the word "employee" in his presence, for example, and you'll get a five-minute lecture: "We don't have employees here. It reduces people to a category and carries with it undertones of ownership. People work at MBNA. And they're not my people, they're their own people. And, happily, they have chosen to work at MBNA. We do not manage these people. We manage their efforts. The people of MBNA are treated as customers and they, in turn, 're-create' that example for external customers."

Cawley's philosophy of business success is neatly summarized in the first statement in MBNA's long-range plan: "The compelling principle on which MBNA America's present and future rests is an unswerving belief that success is essentially the result of an unrelenting pursuit of customer satisfaction. Customer satisfaction means quality."

There is no mistaking the fact that customer satisfaction is an obsession at MBNA. Each month, independent researchers interview 1,100 randomly selected customers to find out how the company is doing. Their findings consistently conclude that MBNA's service meets or exceeds customer expectations 97 percent of the time. And nobody at MBNA thinks that is good enough.

"Unlike a manufacturer that controls the product's lasting quality, our job really doesn't start until after the card reaches the customer," Cawley says. "From that point on, the customer dictates the circumstances under which we 'manufacture' the 'product.' Whenever the customer reaches for our card to make a purchase, our product must be manufactured and delivered on the spot, and at MBNA, that happens well over 125 million times a year."

MBNA's obsession with satisfying customers manifests itself in improved bottom-line results. MBNA has a 95 percent customer-retention rate, 7 percent better than the industry average, a competitive advantage that translates into millions of dollars of added income every year. Its net credit losses are about half of those experienced by VISA.

The company has created a customer-retention SWAT team, staffed by sixty-eight of its best telemarketers, who call customers who cancel to find out why and then try to coax potential defectors back into the fold. They are successful about 50 percent of the time.

Cawley sees all the effort as an imperative for survival. "We've assembled a customer population that includes the most demanding group of people in this country," Cawley says. "Our Gold Card customer is, on average, a professional in his or her mid-forties, making $75,000 or more per year. For example, one-third of all physicians in the country carry our card. This is a group that knows what good service is. They expect it, and they won't settle for anything else."

You know something extraordinary is going on from the moment you set foot inside any of four entrances to MBNA's sprawling facility just outside Wilmington and are greeted by a 9½ × 5½-foot legend, THE CUSTOMER FIRST, woven into the gray and green carpeting. From any point within the sprawling, 500,000-square-foot facility, look in any direction and you'll see a motivational message gently nudging you from the wall, the most ubiquitous being THINK OF YOURSELF AS A CUSTOMER, which is emblazoned above all of the company's 350 doorways.

Because the light and airy complex—the original portion of which was once a supermarket—has only three floors, it has spread out horizontally as the company's needs have grown, and people walk from area to area. This gives the place the feeling of a small, bustling community in which everybody knows everybody but is just a little too busy to chat right now.

There are some highly visible perks—a gym, a day-care center—but management makes it clear that these things exist to encourage quality performance, not simply as altruistic gestures. MBNA is clearly no country club—people are expected to work hard to satisfy the bank's demanding customers. The company recently received over 10,000 unsolicited applications for 750 job openings.

During their first month on the job, every new MBNA person, regardless of position, attends the Customer College, primarily an awareness program designed to make certain that all new people understand that the existence of the company rests on customer satisfaction.

MBNA has a tough measurement program and a generous reward system for meeting performance standards. Special bulletin boards throughout the facility show daily performance levels in fourteen key customer areas. The company puts a significant amount of money into a kitty each day that a 97 percent standard is met and throws in a bonus when the standard is met five days in a row. All non-officers, including part-timers, are rewarded quarterly.

"Tracking of this type is not effective unless it reflects an abiding belief in the importance of providing faultless service," Cawley says. "Belief in good service can make good service happen. Measurement without belief won't move you an inch ahead in the race to quality improvement."

Daily absenteeism at MBNA America is less than 1 percent, and annualized people turnover is 5 percent, less than one-fifth the industry average and staggeringly better than competitors located within a mile of the facility. More than 70 percent of the new people hired are recommended by current MBNA people.

In the end, Cawley believes that if you hire people who like people and treat them fairly they will communicate these values to customers and that, in turn, is what leads to business success.

"People who work in an environment of respect treat customers with respect," Cawley says. "And people who are treated fairly treat customers fairly. This positive environment is reflected in the company's relationship with its customers. By putting the customer first, MBNA America has established the foundation for achieving its primary business objective: 100 percent customer satisfaction—100 percent of the time."

A final note: When MBNA went public on January 29, 1991, it adopted the trading symbol KRB—the initials of Kenneth R. Bowman, former head of quality assurance, who died in May 1990.

INNOVATORS HAVE BIG DREAMS

Jiminy Cricket said it best: "When you wish upon a star, your dreams come true." Attend "The Disney Approach to People Management" seminar at Disney World in Orlando and the first thing you'll hear is that everyone who works anywhere needs an intangible goal—a dream, something bigger than what they do. For Disney, the dream—creating happiness for others for profit—is an enormous business. Since Disney World opened its gates on what was 27,443 acres of Florida swampland in 1972, it has hosted more than 250 million guests—more than the entire population of the United

States—and become the world's most popular tourist destination. More than 300 million people have visited the much smaller Disneyland in California since it opened in 1955. Nearly 70 percent of the guests at Disney theme parks are repeat visitors.

That, as Jiminy might say, is an awful lot of pixie dust to be swept up. At Disney theme parks, cleanliness is the moral equivalent of war. Every Disney World park street surface is whisked clean at least once every fifteen minutes. A custodial staff of 2,000 works round the clock every day of the year. Among their jobs is to steam-clean every piece of pavement and wash every window every day. At Disneyland, workers wear out more than 1,000 brooms, 500 dustpans, and 3,000 mops each year removing 12 million pounds of trash.

In a business where one rude encounter can spoil a family vacation that has been planned for years, getting employees to buy into the dream is tantamount to survival. No company works harder at making its dream tangible to workers. Disney has no quality department, and no one goes through a formal quality-training program. But there is training—and more training. It begins for everyone, regardless of title or position, on his or her first day of employment, with a one-week program called Traditions. This is where the magic begins.

The training focuses on values, history, philosophy, and the dream. Everyone starts with a comprehensive understanding of the dream. It is depicted on the walls from start to future, from motion pictures to the diversity of image engineering, product marketing, and new theme parks. So successful has the company been in managing service quality that it now offers regular seminars on quality and people management to other companies anxious to learn the Disney secrets.

At Disney theme parks, every "cast member" has a name tag—no last names (except in Japan, where last names are permitted because of the strong cultural need for formality and structure), no titles, no variation in size. Length-of-service pins with the ubiquitous mouse in silver or gold are the only deviation permitted.

Disney's rapidly growing "cast," which now numbers more than 75,000 people worldwide, includes 1,500 job descriptions, from accountant to zoologist. They have all been through the Traditions program. There is no mission statement, only a general objective: the finest entertainment for all people of all ages . . . everywhere. The Four Disciplines that deliver the promise are: courtesy, show, efficiency, and safety.

At Disney World, safety is the first priority. Courtesy is second. The operative words are, "What can we do to make you happy?" (not satisfied, but happy). No one is allowed to say, "It's against our policy." What they can say when the guest makes a request (or demand) beyond the practice or standard is, "Let me get a supervisor to help resolve this problem."

Show is third. This discipline includes all elements of the entertainment—the cleanliness, the precision, the attention to detail down to and including the smells.

And efficiency is last. This fact is certainly not reflected in the company's financial performance. Park revenues were $2.6 billion in 1989, accounting for about 60 percent of the company's $4.8 billion in total revenues.

Disney president Frank Wells believes that the heart of the Disney dream is making the intangible tangible. "There must be a daily commitment to excellence that people take with them to work each morning. We see that there is, so that our guests and customers can take home a feeling of quality each night."

INNOVATORS MAKE QUALITY PART OF THEIR CORPORATE VALUES

Consider this record of innovation: Merck & Co. produces eighteen drugs that have worldwide sales of more than $100 million a year. Fourteen of those drugs have been introduced since 1978. No company in the prescription drug industry has ever had that many big winners at the same time.

Led by Roy Vagelos, a physician and biochemist who sometimes refers to the financial and legal sides of the corporation as "all that crap," Merck spent $755 million, or about 11 percent of sales, on R&D in 1989.

In a business that is incredibly quality sensitive, the company has pursued the goal of total quality assurance longer and more passionately than almost anyone. It is certainly no accident that

Merck is consistently ranked as "America's most admired" company in *Fortune*'s annual poll of senior executives.

At Merck, quality is not a program but a legacy, passed down for more than a century by successive generations of key company executives. Continuous improvement is simply part of Merck's culture. For companies that have recently joined the quality bandwagon, these words spoken by the national sales manager of Sharp & Dohme—a forerunner of the current organization—in 1912 to newly hired field sales representatives are instructive indeed:

> Our business was founded in 1860 on the bedrock of Quality. Every brick in our business is a Quality brick. We have preached and practiced Quality for over fifty-two years. And we intend to keep everlastingly at it on the same line for the next fifty-two years, and then begin all over again. True, all of us may not be Sharp & Dohme banner bearers by that time, but our successors will perhaps thank us for laying such a good groundwork. Our most successful salesmen preach Quality persistently and it pays them and the house. Follow suit.

Reinforcing this quality culture has been a major priority for many years. At the company's Merck Sharp & Dohme (MSD) division, for example, virtually all new potential management employees in the operations area begin their careers as quality control inspectors, regardless of their previous background and technical experience. This policy, which has been in effect for more than thirty years, requires each new hire to enter an intensive five-week orientation and training cycle that stresses MSD quality philosophy and specific measurements to safeguard that quality in all the company's products.

MSD's highly acclaimed Pride in Quality program, launched in 1965, is the longest-running zero-defect program in existence throughout American industry.

The lesson of Merck is that quality and customer satisfaction are not fads or programs to be replaced by next year's flavor-of-the-month panacea for poor performance. Quality is a value and continuous improvement is a way of doing business.

Former president George W. Merck—the last Merck to head the company—stated the company's philosophy eloquently at Founder's Day at the University of Virginia in 1950: "We try to remember that medicine is for the patients. It is not for the profits. The profits follow, and if we have remembered that, they have never failed to appear. The better we have remembered it, the larger they have been."

Innovators Don't Compromise Their Quality Standards

McDonald's is known throughout the world for its consistent high standards of quality, service, cleanliness and value. A Big Mac consumed in São Paulo tastes pretty much like a Big Mac consumed in San Francisco. When the giant food service chain opened its first outlet in Moscow in 1989, many people wondered if it could pull off the magic in a country whose food distribution system seems to have been designed by Franz Kafka and where rudimentary service is simply rude. The answer is nothing less than a miracle in Pushkin Square.

Originally designed to serve 15,000 people a day, the massive establishment is now getting upwards of 50,000 eager Soviet customers daily. By 9:30 every morning, a queue of 500 or more people has already formed in front of the brightly lit restaurant located just a few blocks from the Kremlin.

When the doors open at 10, the surging crowds are treated to what is almost certainly the USSR's first attempt at customer satisfaction. The young workers, donning beatific smiles, applaud for the customers as they come through the doors and motion for them to come forward.

George Cohon, president and CEO of McDonald's Canada, and the man whose tenacity brought the Moscow venture to fruition through fourteen years of Soviet red tape, says the morning ritual is something the workers invented on their own. In a country where basic courtesy is an almost unheard-of concept, it has a dramatic effect.

"We are really honored to have a chance to play a role in the development of these kids," Cohon says. "The work ethic they learn at McDonald's will be useful to them no matter what career they go into. McDonald's is not a corporation that comes into a country just to make money. We have always looked to get involved in the fabric of a country because we feel it's critical to our success."

McDonald's realized early on that ensuring a reliable flow of quality supplies would be a major challenge in the Soviet environment. Some analysts estimate that nearly half of all food supplies are spoiled or disappear on the way to the marketplace. While that may be high, chronic shortages of virtually everything are a way of life in the Soviet Union.

The company's solution is McComplex, a vertically integrated, 10,000-square-meter production and distribution facility located in Solntsevo, a suburb forty-five minutes southwest of central Moscow. This is where all the ingredients that go into making a meal at Moscow McDonald's are prepared—according to the same quality standards the chain maintains everywhere else in the world. Of the $50 million it cost to get the Moscow venture off the ground, $40 million went into the Solntsevo facility.

The plant employs 260 people, all but a handful of whom are Soviets, and currently makes three 5-ton shipments of food each day to the restaurant. Demand has been so great that original estimates have doubled. At maximum capacity, the plant produces 10,000 meat patties, 14,000 buns, 3,000 liters of milk, and 5,000 apple pies each hour.

McComplex is the first facility of its kind in the world for McDonald's, with its own bakery, dairy, potato-processing line, meat plant, sauce cookers, and vast storage freezers. Spare parts are manufactured on site, as well, to eliminate long waits should a machine need repair. All raw materials and finished products undergo strict quality control testing before any of the food is shipped to the store.

McDonald's greatest contribution to the state of quality assurance in the Soviet Union may be its working relationship with its suppliers. The company buys virtually all of its raw materials from Soviet producers, no mean feat in a country where much of the food is rationed and quality control is nonexistent. To get around these problems, McDonald's imported potato and cucumber seeds from the Netherlands and trained Soviet farmers to harvest and pack the product without bruising it. They have taught cattle farmers how to increase per-animal yields and to ensure the high-quality beef McDonald's is known for.

Founder Ray Kroc based his philosophy on the idea that consumers wanted Quality food, good Service, Cleanliness, and good Value: Q, S, C, and V. The Moscow experience demonstrates that it is a winning formula that travels anywhere.

INNOVATORS INNOVATE

A popular saying around Minnesota Mining and Manufacturing Company, or 3M as it calls itself these days, is, "You have to kiss a lot of frogs to find a prince." The company, which produces more than forty-five product lines in more than forty divisions around the globe, has always ranked near the top of the world's most innovative companies, so it is no surprise that the $13 billion maker of such ubiquitous consumer products as Scotch tape and Post-It notes has one of the most advanced environmental programs in American industry.

Since 1975, when it launched its Pollution Prevention Pays campaign, the company says 2,511 individual 3P programs have saved $500 million—$426 million in the United States and $74 million overseas.

The 3P program was based for many years on initiatives at the plant level, but in 1989 the company introduced 3P Plus, a more structured corporate effort. The plan calls for each of the company's forty product-operating divisions to develop plans to minimize waste and increase recycling. These efforts are monitored at the corporate level by a pollution-prevention group. Achieving environmental goals has become part of the criteria used in annual performance reviews for managers.

Few, if any, other companies have so successfully melded their environmental strategy into all layers of management and production. Among the elements in the 3M program:

• Building environmentally sound processes into product design and manufacturing to ensure that new processes are as clean as possible. Achieving this goal is greatly enhanced by another 3M objective: to have 25 percent of each division's sales come from products introduced in the last five years. That means production processes are revamped often, allowing the latest and most advanced pollution-reducing technology to be installed.

• The company has committed itself to invest $150 million by 1993 in state-of-the-art pollution-control equipment for its older plants, a move that should reduce emissions by 70 to 75 percent from 1987 levels. Its stated goal is to reduce all emissions from the 1987 base by 90 percent by 2000.

• Although it could sell Federal pollution-reduction credits, 3M has pledged not to do so, saying that it wants to reduce pollution overall, not simply allow other companies to do it.

• The company is using its environmental expertise as a competitive weapon, offering to help customers reduce their own waste problems by taking back some of its packaging.

"Today consumers are speaking to industry and what they are saying is that they intend to vote their dollars to those companies that best meet their needs and quality standards *and* are committed to cleaning up and preserving the environment," says Douglas Anderson, 3M's director of quality. "It's a message that's too important to be ignored."

INNOVATORS INVOLVE EMPLOYEES IN THE DESIGN OF WORK

Before 1989, US Healthcare, the largest independent health maintenance organization (HMO) in the country, was known for its skill in marketing its services and for providing good managed health care through a reliable network of independent physicians.

The company had also developed a reputation for being a pioneer in studying the practices of physicians and incorporating quality standards that measured their effectiveness and rewarded those with the highest levels of performance. Among its innovations:

• A system for physician selection and compensation that includes an intensive screening process plus an ongoing system for "grading" physicians and giving them annual report cards.

• Analytical software to measure quality of physician services and outcome of medical procedures.

• Warranties for specific medical procedures such as liptho-tripsy, organ replacement, and cardiac surgery.

• The most ambitious preventive health care program in the industry aimed at keeping members healthy and enhancing the quality of their lives.

• Formation of a new company—USQA—whose mission is to develop analytical tools to measure and assess quality as it relates to delivery of health care services.

• Establishment of the U.S. Healthcare Quality Achievement to recognize individuals and organizations in the area of quality delivery of health care.

Internally, however, the company was something of a casualty of its own success. Founded by president and CEO Leonard Abramson just a few years after the passage of the HMO Act of 1973, the company grew rapidly and converted to for-profit status in 1982. In 1989, US Healthcare topped $1 billion in revenues and signed on its one millionth member.

"Our operations areas—those areas that process the paper—were struggling to keep up with the growth," Abramson says. "Turnover rates in people were 40 percent to 60 percent a year. The knowledge needed to do work was leaving the business faster than new people could be hired. Consequently, follow-through on customer issues and problems was often incomplete. Systems developed to correct errors and support services were less than effective due to quality problems in the data entered. These were clearly problems that no business can afford or survive."

The company chose continuous improvement as the vehicle to build a quality renaissance. Goals that people could relate to were established. Communication lines were identified and opened. Computer systems that were better able to support required work were engineered. A "Vital Signs" quality standards and measurement system was implemented with a healthy reward system that included all people who support the customer. "Image Building" training was introduced to inform, impart knowledge, and create a sense of purpose and worth in the work force.

Perhaps the most dramatic example of the change was the process the U.S. company followed in designing its member service facility in Blue Bell, Pennsylvania. For more than six months, an eighteen-person team of employees called the Vision Builders—representing every department and discipline—met weekly to help develop what the company believes is the best customer service center in the health care industry and a model for all other businesses that provide customer service.

"We put the Vision Builders program in place because we wanted all of our employees to have the opportunity to participate and help us achieve a vision of excellence together," says Marcy Abramson, vice president and director of operations. "In today's corporate environment, there is still a great deal of structure and rigidity. Everyone works in their own area and doesn't see the larger picture. Vision Builders is a conscious effort to break down the barriers. We are saying to US Healthcare employees: 'This is your company. You can make a mark. You can contribute to everything that goes on here.' "

The Vision Builders were assigned specific projects—a new computer and phone system, work function layout, signage, and design—based on their specific areas of expertise. However, the aim was for employees from all disciplines to have a say when it comes to key issues that will affect the total environment.

The results of this teamwork approach were nothing short of revolutionary: a building designed not only to facilitate but to play an active role in promoting the company's vision and philosophy; offices with no doors and almost no paper; technology that allows employees to know when a customer is calling and have the information ready to answer his or her question even before the telephone is picked up; an electronic display—similar to the readout from a heart monitor—that graphically shows how the company's people are meeting key service standards; a personnel department called Star Search; and a corporate training department called Image Building.

The net effect of the company's quality initiative was immediately apparent. Turnover in 1990 dropped to less than 9 percent, a dramatic improvement in the first year.

"The foundation of any company's success rests with its people," said Abramson. "Good, hardworking people, who bring skill, ingenuity, and determination to any task set before them. We took this belief to heart and charged our people with creating a customer service 'Workplace for the Future.' They ran with the challenge and helped us create an atmosphere that emphasizes, facilitates, and rewards customer service."

INNOVATORS LEARN FROM EXPERIENCE

The most persuasive—and controversial—illustration that Japanese-style quality management can work in America is the Fremont, California, plant run by New United Motor Manufacturing Inc. (NUMMI), a joint venture between General Motors and Toyota. Organized in 1983 and launched in 1984 through a historic agreement between the two auto companies and the United Auto Workers—in a plant where labor relations were so bad that it had been closed by GM—NUMMI has received national and international recognition for its world-class quality and innovative approaches to people management. The plant uses the Toyota production system and produces cars according to the needs of its parent companies.

The results have been spectacular. In an MIT study of automobile quality, NUMMI rated 135 to 140 out of a possible score of 145. Labor productivity is at least 50 percent higher than at other GM plants and almost as high as that of Japanese Toyota plants. It takes NUMMI workers twenty hours to assemble a car, versus twenty-eight hours for a comparable auto at a GM plant. Absenteeism is about 2 percent, versus 9 percent at a typical GM factory.

UAW officials like to point out that 85 percent of NUMMI's employees worked at the Fremont plant before the joint venture was created—a fact that seems to suggest that management was the problem before the change.

Leaving aside the matter of blame, there is little doubt that the NUMMI approach is radically different from that followed in most American companies. The following seven goals, excerpted from the NUMMI team member handbook, illustrate just how different.

1. *Kaizen: The Never-Ending Quest for Perfection. Kaizen* is a tool in "the search for constant improvement in self, team, NUMMI, and community."

2. *Develop Full Human Potential.* "Progress in the automobile

industry, as in any industry, is built upon the dreams and sweat of men, and the perseverance to conquer difficulties that seem, at times, overwhelming to the strongest."

3. *Pursuit of Superior Quality.* "If we are designing a new product, our attitude certainly must not be just to aim for the average. We must all do our best at all times."

4. *Build Mutual Trust.* "There is nothing more important than being faithful to one's trust. If you follow that principle your heart will always be at rest."

5. *Develop Team Performance.* "Let each of us strive whole-heartedly to fulfill the trust placed in us in the execution of our duties. Just as a chain is made of many links, so in working together do we possess enormous strength."

6. *Every Employee a Manager.* "Good thinking equals good products. Accept responsibility yourself for all matters relating to your company."

7. *Provide a Stable Environment.* "Without ensuring its employees a stable livelihood through sound management, the company understands it cannot hope to enjoy growth and prosperity."

The NUMMI approach reflects the Japanese philosophy that a balanced socio-technical system in which workers are in harmony with machines is the only way to continuously improve the system. Hence every aspect of the plant's operation depends upon the smooth functioning of everything else. Four key interrelated systems bind this approach together:

• *Collaborative Problem Solving* is the mechanism used for building consensus and approaching problems before they reach disastrous proportions. Regularly involving all parties affected by a problem and using the solutions that evolve from the collaborative process enhance both the understanding of the problem and commitment to its solution.

• *Jikoda* is the method for establishing harmony between workers and machines and product and process. At NUMMI, team members control the production line to assure quality. This team control is a first for American industry and is written into the labor-management agreement.

• *Just-in-Time* sharply improves the flow of work and material and gives workers a sense of control and a sense of responsibility for the next step in the process.

• *Total Quality Control* is a formal company-wide commitment to continuous improvement.

The key insight is that each of these systems is related to, and dependent upon, the others for the orderly functioning of the factory. One of the mistakes that many American companies made in trying to improve quality during the 1980s was to adopt one or another of these elements while ignoring the rest.

Not everyone agrees that NUMMI is a workers' paradise. Former auto workers Mike Parker and Jane Slaughter, authors of *Choosing Sides: Unions and the Team Concept,* call the NUMMI approach "management by stress" and say that the plant's enhanced productivity is due less to employee involvement or sharing of work than to tight control of the work force.

"In fact, NUMMI has achieved its gains through far greater regimentation of the work force than exists in traditional auto plants," they write. "Tight specifications and monitoring of how jobs are to be done, a barebones work force with no replacements for absentees and a systematic and continuing speedup are the methods used."[4]

Bruce Lee, director of the UAW's western region, who was involved in the NUMMI negotiations, vociferously disagrees: "The lessons of NUMMI's success are still being resisted by executives, plant managers, and foremen who see their authority threatened by the idea of power-sharing," he says. "It is also resisted by a few old-guard unions who are uncomfortable with the idea of sharing responsibility with management for the plant's success in the marketplace. NUMMI and the UAW have also been the targets of a political disinformation campaign by a handful of 1960s-era leftists who are still hanging around the fringes of the trade union movement. These aging 'revolutionaries' never imagined this kind of revolution."[5]

The truth probably lies somewhere between these extremes. What is indisputable is that the NUMMI approach boosts productivity and quality. Despite its critics, it is emerging as a model for world-class manufacturing and labor relations.

GM has already applied many of the lessons of NUMMI to its new Saturn plant in Spring Hill, Tennessee, which began producing its first models in late 1990. Saturn was specifically designed to produce automobiles that would appeal to the segment of the American driving public that has come to prefer Japanese cars.

Under an innovative agreement drawn up in 1984 by union and GM representatives, Saturn managers and workers agreed to share information, authority, and decision making. That means that the ranking union official at the plant works on roughly the same level as Saturn's president. They both attend the same meetings, are privy to the same information, and have a say in top-level decisions.

The working format at Saturn is radically different from that used in conventional American auto plants. Regular workers, not specialists, are responsible for casting parts and machining them into their final shape, a process that requires more training and higher levels of skill. They also have final responsibility for quality.

The Saturn plant also makes extensive use of quality function deployment (QFD) to engineer in features that are identified as customer requirements. For example, engineers used the process to identify 14,000 variables that can be controlled in the manufacture of a transmission; they then narrowed their search for improvements down to the 200 that are most important to customers. To help in the process, the company keeps Honda and Accura test vehicles in the plant so workers and engineers can stay in close touch with the products they're trying to beat.

No one wears ties at Saturn, and the lines between "blue collar" and "white collar" are deliberately blurred. All workers are paid a salary rather than an hourly wage, and all will eventually be awarded a bonus or penalized, proportionate to their annual wages, depending upon the plant's profitability. Early reports from Saturn suggest that both workers and managers like the less rigid approach being used at Saturn and that the models being produced do, indeed, perform as well as the Japanese models they are intended to imitate.

INNOVATORS HAVE A VISION AND A STRATEGY TO MAKE IT HAPPEN

When John F. (Jack) Welch, Jr., took over the helm of General Electric in 1981 at the age of forty-five, the youngest CEO in

GE's history, he inherited a sprawling bureaucracy of 348 businesses or product lines, many of them marginal performers, and 400,000 employees. By the end of the 1980s, GE was a finely tuned company of fourteen divisions, with products ranging from light bulbs and aircraft engines to major appliances and TV broadcasting. One quarter of its work force—100,000 people—were gone through attrition, layoffs, and the sale of businesses.

Not surprisingly, Welch is often cited as one of America's most "ruthless" business leaders and has earned the nickname "Neutron Jack" (the buildings are still standing but the people are gone).

What is seldom said is that Welch is one of the very few American business leaders who has made a change program actually produce change. In the process, he may have saved the aging company from extinction.

GE entered the 1980s ranked eleventh in marketing value at $12 billion and ended them second in market value at $58 billion—the biggest value increase of any American company during the decade. Productivity tripled and the company had forty consecutive quarters of earnings increases.

Welch's vision was a simple one: a line of business had to be number one or number two in its industry or out it went. Little wonder that Welch's favorite management thinker is Helmuth von Moltke, a Prussian general who served as a military adviser to the Ottoman court—the nineteenth-century equivalent of a management consultant. In a *Fortune* interview, Welch said: "Von Moltke believed strategy was not a lengthy action plan but rather the evolution of a central idea through continually changing circumstances."[6]

One idea that has been central to Welch's thinking is the importance of quality as a competitive weapon. In a speech to the 1980 GE Marketing Management Conference in Hot Springs, Virginia, Welch, then vice chairman, said: "Quality is not a single thing, but an aura, an atmosphere, an overpowering feeling that a company is doing everything with excellence, and that the customer is elevated, enhanced in his self-worth and image, bettered by his relationship with the company."

By linking quality to customer perceptions, Welch was about ten years ahead of most American business leaders, who are only now beginning to discover the value of a quality image.

The first policy Welch put in place as the incoming CEO in 1981 was directed at quality *and* personal responsibility—a theme that has obsessed him and guided his vision at GE. Prior to the Welch era, the role of the corporate staff was to "cross-check" operations. Internal memos report that "collection of quality data was one facet of this philosophy of identifying signs of trouble that could be used by central authority to measure operational performance." The new policy was designed to eliminate "the protracted waiting and eventual goading from a remote bureaucratic authority" and put the immediate responsibility on local management to determine quality measures most relevant to that specific business. The policy reads:

> *Company Policy Number 20.1*
>
> It is the policy of General Electric, in offering products and services that fill a wide range of customers' needs, to pursue and deserve a reputation for quality leadership, and to merit customer trust because full value is being received.
>
> It is the policy of General Electric, in fulfilling its social responsibilities and in every aspect of its relationships both outside and inside the company, to demonstrate total dedication to the attainment of quality leadership.

Eight years after the 1981 policy statement, GE's annual report said:

> We want . . . to become a company where people come to work every day in a rush to try something they woke up thinking about the night before. We want them to go home from work wanting to talk about what they did that day, rather than trying to forget about it. We want factories where the whistle blows and everyone wonders where the time went, and someone suddenly wonders aloud why we need a whistle. We want a company where people find a better way, every day, of doing things; and where by shaping their own work experience, they make their lives better and your Company best.
>
> Far-fetched? Fuzzy? Soft? Naive? Not a bit. This is the type of liberated, involved, excited, boundary-less culture that is

present in successful start-up enterprises. It is unheard of in an institution our size; but we want it, and we are determined we will have it.

Clearly, the evolution of a central idea is evident. With restructuring behind him, Welch has articulated a new, kinder, gentler vision for the 1990s. He calls it Speed, Simplicity, and Self-Confidence and it is clearly designed to boost GE's productivity.

"We found in the '80s that becoming faster is tied to becoming simpler," Welch says. "Our businesses, most with tens of thousands of employees, will not respond to visions that have sub-paragraphs and footnotes. If we're not simple we can't be fast . . . and if we can't be fast we can't win."

To engage the hearts and minds of its workers and managers, the company has launched a new war on waste called Work-Out. Its philosophical underpinning is continuous improvement. As Welch puts it, Work-Out is "a relentless, endless, company-wide search for a better way to do everything we do," and it is "designed to create an environment where every man and woman in the company can see and feel a connection between what he or she does all day . . . and winning in the marketplace . . . the ultimate job security."

An important part of the Work-Out program is open sessions, reminiscent of New England town meetings, where GE people are encouraged to talk about anything that gets in the way of doing good work: bureaucracy, autocracy, paperwork, reports, non-value added cycles and procedures. Everyone participates, including suppliers and customers, but it is mainly GE's employees who are asked to contribute. Other elements of the program are benchmarking and simplification of design and manufacturing processes.

If Jack Welch has any regrets about the cultural revolution he has wrought at GE, he keeps them to himself. As the supremely self-confident chemical engineer turned corporate revolutionary puts it: "We had constructed over the years a management apparatus that was right for its times, the toast of the business schools. Divisions, strategic business units, groups, sectors, all were designed to make meticulous, calculated decisions and move them smoothly forward and upward. This system produces highly polished work. It was right for the '70s . . . a growing handicap in the early '80s . . . and it would have been a ticket to the boneyard in the '90s."

A Final Thought

How do you end a book on continuous improvement? Could this be the first business book without an ending? As the authors, we know that our improvement process will continue and that by the time this book is published our thoughts and experiences will have produced newer ideas and notions that embellish and extend the argument, the rationale, the evidence.

We thought of ending the book by creating a composite quality company—taking the best ideas and people from the companies that we have written about and putting them together in model fashion. We started the exercise but did not get too far. We abandoned the idea when we realized that the unique character of each company, those we have reported on and those we have not yet gotten to know, makes it special and defies the notion of a model.

Those companies that are driven by an obsession with improvement, that support and embrace each employee's value and contribution, and that focus on the changing needs of their customers create a special brand of quality that results in personal satisfaction, pride, and good work. Getting beyond quality will require even greater perseverance.

Afterword

The Ten Commandments of Continuous Improvement

The companies that survive and prosper in the 1990s will be those that diligently pursue continuous improvement in the holy trinity of business survival: quality, customer focus, and innovation. The stakes are high. As Lester Thurow put it at a Xerox Quality Conference in 1990: "On the stroke of midnight on December 31, 1992, the United States will become the second-largest economy in the world for the first time in a century."[1]

More than corporate profits are at risk; the challenge is to the American standard of living.

The companies profiled in this book have demonstrated that American companies can compete, and compete well, if they are wise enough to learn and remember the hard lessons of the 1980s. Those lessons make up what we call The Ten Commandments of Continuous Improvement:

1. *Put the customer first.* Without customers, there is no business. Companies must focus first and foremost on fulfilling the ever-changing expectations of the marketplace in such a manner that they earn and keep the trust of their customers.

2. *Innovate constantly.* But do not emphasize product innova-

tion over process innovation. Breakthroughs are important, but incremental improvements to succeeding generations of products and services are just as important.

3. *Design quality into products and services;* plan for prevention. Stopping defects before they happen is more productive and cost-effective than detecting them after the fact. By anticipating problems, you can avoid time and costs associated with "inspecting them out" and rework.

4. *Improve everything continually;* quality improvement never ends. All work is part of a process; every process can be improved, no matter how good it is today. An emphasis on continuous improvement fosters creativity and breakthroughs.

5. *Create and support a safe and open work environment* that seeks out, nurtures, rewards, and celebrates the contribution of each employee.

6. *Do not shoot the messenger.* Overcome the barriers to quality and productivity: discuss the undiscussibles.

7. *Stop imitating the Japanese.* Heed this Japanese proverb: The crow, imitating the cormorant, drowns in the water.

8. *Use time wisely.* Speeding up production or delivery cuts costs, accelerates new product development, and improves quality. The fastest way to get something done is to do the right things right the first time.

9. *Do not sacrifice long-term improvements for short-term profits.*

10. *Quality is not enough.*

Appendix A

1991 Examination Categories and Items
Malcolm Baldrige National Quality Award

1991 Examination Categories/Items	Maximum Points	
1.0 Leadership		100
1.1 Senior Executive Leadership	40	
1.2 Quality Values	15	
1.3 Management for Quality	25	
1.4 Public Responsibility	20	
2.0 Information and Analysis		70
2.1 Scope and Management of Quality Data and Information	20	
2.2 Competitive Comparisons and Benchmarks	30	
2.3 Analysis of Quality Data and Information	20	
3.0 Strategic Quality Planning		60
3.1 Strategic Quality Planning Process	35	
3.2 Quality Goals and Plans	25	
4.0 Human Resource Utilization		150
4.1 Human Resource Management	20	
4.2 Employee Involvement	40	

4.3 Quality Education and Training	40
4.4 Employee Recognition and Performance Measurement	25
4.5 Employee Well–Being and Morale	25
5.0 Quality Assurance of Products and Services	**140**
5.1 Design and Introduction of Quality Products and Services	35
5.2 Process Quality Control	20
5.3 Continuous Improvement of Processes	20
5.4 Quality Assessment	15
5.5 Documentation	10
5.6 Business Process and Support Service Quality	20
5.7 Supplier Quality	20
6.0 Quality Results	**180**
6.1 Product and Service Quality Results	90
6.2 Business Process, Operational, and Support Service Quality Results	50
6.3 Supplier Quality Results	40
7.0 Customer Satisfaction	**300**
7.1 Determining Customer Requirements and Expectations	30
7.2 Customer Relationship Management	50
7.3 Customer Service Standards	20
7.4 Commitment to Customers	15
7.5 Complaint Resolution for Quality Improvement	25
7.6 Determining Customer Satisfaction	20
7.7 Customer Satisfaction Results	70
7.8 Customer Satisfaction Comparison	70
TOTAL POINTS	1000

Don't Even Think of Changing the Baldrige Criteria: How to Read the Recommended Improvements

In New York (where we work and play) it is almost impossible to find a parking space. Any open space is an invitation to park, regardless of prohibitions or the dictates of common courtesy. In fact, people trying to protect their driveways have replaced "no parking" signs with the stronger imperative: "Don't even **think** of parking here!" The same implied message is often directed to those who want to make changes in the Baldrige criteria. Our belief is that while there is an improvement process built into the criteria, it's not on a scale that is commensurate with the total challenge for improvement in business today. Thus, in the spirit of New York *chutzpa,* we are offering here our Expanded Version of the criteria.

Verbally suggesting changes, as we have done in several public forums, is one thing. Putting them in print—not without some fear and trepidation on our part—is another matter altogether. Our *Beyond Quality* categories are internally consistent with the themes of this book. The keys to reading the chart and making a comparison with the existing Baldrige categories are:

1. Any number, category, or item in **bold type** represents a change or departure from the Baldrige categories.
2. Any asterisk (★) represents an *increase* in the value for the same category in Baldrige.
3. Any double asterisk (★★) represents a *decrease* in the value for the same category in Baldrige.

Clues and rationales for why we have added categories and items, and deleted some of the Baldrige items, are to be found throughout this book, especially in the latter chapters. For example, under Leadership we have added Vision, because we have seen the power it has in companies like Disney and General Electric (which have not yet applied and possibly may not apply for the Baldrige Award), and we have come to appreciate the role that vision plays in creating an "impossible dream"—a key ingredient in the American quality archetype study referenced in Chapter 9.

Another example is "personal applications by CEO"—notice that our recommendation is specific, not a general reference to "senior management." We feel that the criteria should demand that the leadership of Baldrige applicants personally apply the quality improvement process to their administrative and management responsibilities. A role model here is Jamie Houghton at Corning, who understands that his personal secretary is one of his key "customers" whom he needs to satisfy with clarity of instructions so that she can do her job right the first time. Houghton has also changed the structure of his management meetings based on quality improvement concepts.

Finally, under Leadership we have an item on "closing the rhetoric gap." What is that? It is the discrepancy that employees see between what a CEO says is important and what a CEO does to follow up. This gap, for Baldrige applicants, would be measured by opinion surveys of employees.

Another example of our rationale is under Human Resource Utilization, where our proposal is simple and straightforward: one point for each percent of employees who say they are involved in a quality program.

We are probably most vulnerable on Customer Satisfaction, especially since we cut the number of points in half! But we feel that by adding an Innovation category with 150 points, we have more than compensated for the cut. After all, innovation is what is going to *keep* customers "satisfied." We also make up for the cut by doubling the points and adding items in Leadership to strengthen the value of this category. And (maybe we are being too defensive) the separate category for Public Responsibility brings the larger customer— society—into proper focus. After all, customers are those you have and those you want. If you "satisfy" the larger customer, your marketing efforts should have a higher return in the long run. Think environmental accountability, for example.

One improvement strategy that might sit better in Washington is a Bonus Category. Keep the categories as they are, but add a bonus of 100 points or so for, say, Innovation. That might work as well.

Beyond Quality: Suggested Examination Categories and Items for the Baldrige Award

1.0 Leadership	200
1.1 Vision	25
1.2 Senior executive leadership	40
1.3 Quality values	40★
1.4 Personal applications by CEO	20
1.5 Closing the rhetoric gap	75
2.0 Long-term planning	**100**
2.1 Management by fact	25
2.2 Five-year plan	25
2.3 Ten-year plan	50
3.0 Human Resource Utilization	150
3.1 Employee involvement **(one point for each percent involved)**	100★
3.2 Employee education and training	50★
4.0 Quality Assurance of Products and Services	100★★
4.1 Design	50★
4.2 Use of the quality tools	25
4.3 Supplier quality	25★
5.0 Customer Satisfaction	150★★
5.1 Determining customer requirements	30
5.2 Determining market expectations	20
5.3 Complaint management and resolution	50★
5.4 Customer satisfaction results	50★
6.0 Innovation	150
6.1 Cycle time reduction	65
6.2 Value added design	25
6.3 Research & Development budget	10
6.4 Product/service innovations	25
6.5 Process innovations	25
7.0 Financial performance	**50**
7.1 Integration of quality functions	25
7.2 Cost savings from process improvements	25

8.0 Public Responsibility   100

8.1	Policy statements on ethics, public health and safety, environment, and waste management	25
8.2	Integration of the improvement process	25
8.3	Employee education and training	25
8.4	Participation in community	25
	TOTAL POINTS	1000

Appendix B

A Field Guide to the Quality Gurus

PHILIP B. CROSBY

Philip B. Crosby is founder of the Quality College in Winter Park, Florida, and author of many books, including the influential 1979 bestseller *Quality Is Free*. The son of a West Virginia foot doctor, who favors flashy ties and big rings, Crosby is often dismissed as a lightweight by more intellectual quality professionals (including Deming), who say he is a "motivator" who lacks a "methodology." This is mostly sour grapes, occasioned by the fact that Crosby was among the first quality professionals to hold a senior management position (vice president for quality at ITT from 1965 to 1979, under the estimable Harold Geneen), the fact that he was the first "guru" to achieve wide public fame through his writing, and the fact that he has almost certainly made more money from quality improvement consulting than anyone alive.

Crosby's fame began in 1962 when he was quality director of the Martin Company, which was then building Pershing missiles. Like all the other military contractors, Martin found that it could deliver high quality only through a program of rigorous inspection and so-called reliability engineering. At Crosby's suggestion, the manager of Martin's Orlando, Florida, plant decided to offer workers incentives to lower the rate of defects. In December 1961 Martin delivered a Pershing missile with "zero discrepancies." Encouraged by this success, the general manager accepted a challenge from the

Army's missile command to deliver the first field Pershing one month ahead of schedule. He also promised that the missile would have no hardware or document errors, and that all equipment would be fully operational ten days after delivery (the norm was ninety days or more). In February 1962 Martin delivered on time a perfect missile that was fully operational in less than twenty-four hours. From then on, "Zero Defects" became a rallying cry for American industry.

Basic Ideas

• Quality can be caused by deliberate management action. The philosophical basis for the desired quality culture change is outlined by the Four Absolutes of Quality Management:

1. Quality is defined as conformance to requirements.
2. The system for causing quality is prevention.
3. The performance standard is zero defects.
4. The measurement of quality is the price of nonconformance.

• The 14 Step Quality Improvement Process is designed to structure and position the organization for operational improvements and improved communications.

The 14 Steps:

1. Management Commitment
2. Quality Improvement Team
3. Measurement
4. Cost of Quality
5. Awareness
6. Corrective Action
7. Zero Defects Planning
8. Employee Education
9. Zero Defects Day
10. Goal Setting
11. Error Cause Removal
12. Recognition
13. Quality Councils
14. Do It All Again

• According to Crosby, relationships and quality are two keys to successful leadership. A management team must exercise care to avoid viewing relationships and quality as overhead functions that do not contribute directly to profitability.

Relationships: "The ecology of an organization is as delicate and vulnerable as that of a forest. Nothing happens without having an effect on something. The key to all these things within a company, as within a forest is relationships."

Quality: "Quality is the result of a carefully constructed culture; it has to be the fabric of the organization—not part of the fabric, but the actual fabric. It is not hard for a modern management team to produce quality if they are willing to learn how to change and implement."

W. EDWARDS DEMING

The world's best-known quality guru was born in 1900 and grew up on a Wyoming homestead. After working his way through the University of Wyoming, and a master's program at the University of Colorado, he got a Ph.D. in physics from Yale in 1924. While working at the U.S. Department of Agriculture in the 1930s, he met Walter A. Shewhart, who introduced him to statistical control. During the war, he taught statistical quality control to companies involved in wartime production. In 1947 he was recruited by General MacArthur's occupation forces to help Japan prepare for the 1951 census. In 1950 he gave the first of a series of now famous lectures to Japanese industry leaders, leading to the establishment of the Deming Prize. Virtually ignored in his own country, Deming labored in relative obscurity in the U.S. until he was "discovered"— at the age of eighty—through a television documentary, "If Japan Can . . . Why Can't We?"

Basic ideas

Constancy of purpose serves as an agent releasing the power of intrinsic motivation by creating joy, pride, and happiness in work and in learning for all employees. Leadership attributes, attainment of profound knowledge, application of statistical methodologies, understanding and harnessing the sources of variation, and perpetuating a cycle of continuous quality improvement are at the heart of Deming's philosophy. The 14 Points for Management describe the transformation that must be accomplished. Willing workers help make it a reality.

The 14 Points for Management

1. Create constancy of purpose for improvement of product and service.

2. Adopt the new philosophy.
3. Cease dependence on inspection to achieve quality.
4. End the practice of awarding business on the basis of price tag alone. Instead, minimize total cost by working with a single supplier.
5. Improve constantly and forever every process for planning, production, and service.
6. Institute training on the job.
7. Adopt and institute leadership.
8. Drive out fear.
9. Break down barriers between staff areas.
10. Eliminate slogans, exhortations, and targets for the work force.
11. Eliminate numerical quotas for the work force and numerical goals for management.
12. Remove barriers that rob people of pride of workmanship. Eliminate the annual rating or merit system.
13. Institute a vigorous program of education and self-improvement for everybody.
14. Put everybody in the company to work to accomplish the transformation.

ARMAND V. FEIGENBAUM

A. V. Feigenbaum is a leading author, quality consultant, and former manager of manufacturing operations and quality control at General Electric. Feigenbaum joined GE in the late 1930s, just out of high school, and continued to work there during summer vacations while studying engineering at Union College in Schenectady. Among his first jobs was working with GE's engineering group on a priority war effort—the world's first jet engines—which sometimes worked, sometimes didn't. Through statistical and other methods, Feigenbaum's group was able to develop—in a few months—techniques to determine exactly what parts were undependable and why.

In 1944, at age twenty-four, Feigenbaum was named top quality expert for GE in Schenectady. In 1951 he earned a Ph.D. from MIT, and in 1958 he was named manager of manufacturing operations for GE worldwide, a position he held for ten years.

Feigenbaum coined the term "total quality control" in an article in the *Harvard Business Review* in 1956 and published a classic textbook by the same title in 1961. His basic premise was that quality relates to every function and activity within the organization, not simply manufacturing and engineering but also traditional white-collar functions such as marketing and finance. He also invented the concept of "cost of quality." Total Quality Control is defined as the system for integrating the quality development, quality maintenance, and quality improvement efforts of groups in an organization enabling production and service at the most economical levels which allow for full customer satisfaction.

Basic Ideas

The four jobs of quality control are: New Design Control, Incoming Material Control, Product Control, and Special Process Studies.

The subsystems for Total Quality Control

Preproduction Quality Evaluation
Product and Process Quality Planning
Purchased Material Quality Evaluation and Control
Product and Process Quality Evaluation and Control
Quality Information Feedback
Quality Information Equipment
Quality Training, Orientation, and Manpower Development
Postproduction Quality Service
Management of the Quality Control Function
Special Quality Studies

Basic benchmarks of Total Quality Management

- Quality must be structured to support both the quality work of individuals and the quality teamwork among departments.
- Quality must be perceived to be what the buyer says it is—not what the engineer, marketer, or general manager says it is.
- Modern quality improvement requires the application of new technology; it's not a matter of dusting off a few traditional quality control techniques.
- Make quality a full equal partner with innovation from the onset of quality development.
- Emphasize getting high-quality product design and process matches upstream—before design freezes the quality alternatives.
- Make the acceleration of new-product introduction a primary measure of the effectiveness of a quality program.

KAORU ISHIKAWA

Until his death in 1988, Kaoru Ishikawa was president of Musashi Institute of Technology in Tokyo. He previously was professor of engineering at the Science University of Tokyo and the University of Tokyo. Born into an aristocratic Japanese family, Ishikawa was in the forefront of the Japanese quality revolution from its beginnings in the late 1940s. He was awarded the Deming prize in Japan and the Shewhart Medal by the ASQC for "his outstanding contributions to the development of quality control theory, principles, techniques, QC activities, and standardization activities for both Japanese and world industry which enhanced quality and productivity."

Basic ideas

• Total Quality Control (TQC) opens up channels of communication within a company, filling it with a breath of fresh air. TQC allows companies to discover a failure before it turns into a disaster, because everyone is accustomed to speaking to one another truthfully, frankly, and in a helpful manner.

• TQC makes it possible for the product design and manufacturing divisions to follow the changing tastes and attitudes of customers efficiently and accurately so that products can be manufactured to meet customer preference consistently.

• TQC fosters probing minds that can detect false data. It can help companies avoid relying on false sales figures and false production figures. Knowledge Is Power, and that is what TQC can provide.

• The philosophy of company-wide quality assurance emphasizes the customer and societal issues through the following objectives:

Quality First
Not short-term profit first.

Consumer Orientation
Not producer orientation; think from the standpoint of the other party.

The Next Process Is Your Customer
Breaking down the barrier of sectionalism.

Using Facts and Data to Make Presentation
Utilization of statistical methods.

Respect for Humanity as a Management Philosophy
Full participatory management.

Cross-Function Management
The approach used to solve problems.

JOSEPH M. JURAN

Juran's *Quality Control Handbook,* published in 1951, has become the bible of the quality improvement movement in both Japan and the U.S. Born in Rumania in 1904, Juran moved with his family to Minnesota in 1912. He earned an engineering degree from the University of Minnesota, then joined the inspection department— what would now be called quality control—of the Hawthorne Works in 1924. At the time, the Hawthorne plants employed 40,000 people—5,000 of whom worked in inspection. In 1926 he worked with a team from Bell Laboratories to set up the first statistical process control techniques for factories. At the beginning of World War II, Juran joined the Lend-Lease administration. Following the war, he became a consultant and writer, but until McGraw-Hill published his textbook—after it was turned down by several other publishers— Juran had few clients. The book brought him a legion of admirers, none more ardent than the Japanese.

In his book *What Is Total Quality Control?—The Japanese Way,* Ishikawa credits Juran's visit to Japan in 1954 with helping the Japanese change from an effort "dealing primarily with technology, based in factories, to an overall concern for the entire management."

Basic Ideas

- Quality control is analogous to financial control.
- Quality planning is analogous to financial planning and budgeting.
- Quality improvement is analogous to cost reduction.

Juran stresses what he calls the "project approach" to quality improvement, in which problems are identified and then "scheduled for solution." He pioneered the use of Pareto analysis to target prime improvement opportunities by separating the "vital few" from the "useful many."

Basic ideas

- Quality is defined as fitness for use.
- Survival and growth are dependent on "breakthrough" to new levels of performance.

- Customer needs are translated into product and process features.
- Cost of poor quality is the attention-getting tool.
- Chronic waste must be identified and eliminated.
- Pareto analysis is used to target prime improvement opportunities by separating the "vital few" from the "useful many."
- The Quality Trilogy concept provides a universal way of thinking about quality. The elements of The Quality Trilogy are:

Quality Planning
The process for preparing to meet quality goals.

Quality Control
The process for meeting quality goals during operations.

Quality Improvement
The process for breaking through to superior, unprecedented levels of performance.

The role of upper managers

- Accept training in how to manage for quality.
- Create and lead a quality council that guides and coordinates the process through which the company meets its quality goals.
- Personally determine which quality goals should enter the business plan.
- Approve the methods of measurement of quality goals.
- Personally review progress against the goals.
- Participate in recognition ceremonies.
- Approve revisions in the reward system.

Portions of this appendix were adapted from "Total Quality Management: Philosophies and Applications," published by the General Motors Quality Institute.

Appendix C

Scoring Guidelines
President's Award for Quality and Productivity
Improvement

The following scoring guidelines, used by the Federal Quality Institute for a national government quality award that parallels the Baldrige Award, are provided as one way to benchmark progress in quality improvement.

1. TOP MANAGEMENT LEADERSHIP & SUPPORT (20 POINTS)

100–80% • Top executives directly/actively involved in quality-related activities; communicate organization's quality vision, goals, values
- Organization's policy is that TQM is number one priority, key to success; belief in continuous improvement permeates organization; effective strategies used to involve all managers, supervisors in quality
- Management provides significant resources (time, training, dollars) necessary to improve quality throughout organization
- Environment encourages innovation, pride in work,

continuous improvement, open communication (vertically, horizontally), information-sharing, cooperation across departments
- "Ownership" of quality effort assessed, reinforced at all levels
- Long-term top management commitment; no short-term compromises counter to quality
- Top management accessible to/has routine contact with employees, customers, suppliers
- Top management holds everyone accountable for improving systems/processes, products/services; rewards behavior that reflects quality improvement goals
- Managers play active role in removing barriers to excellence
- Extent to which quality values have been adopted throughout organization evaluated on routine basis

---

80–60%
- Top executives participate in Quality Councils, other leadership activities; communicate organization's quality vision, goals, values
- TQM is number one priority of most groups within organization; belief in continuous improvement permeates most of organization; effective strategies used to involve most managers, supervisors in quality
- Adequate resources (time, training, dollars) invested to improve quality throughout organization
- Communications are two-way, clear, consistent; information shared vertically; departments cooperate to achieve continuous improvement
- "Ownership" of quality effort exercised at all levels
- Top management supports long-term quality improvement goals, many quality improvement projects with only long-term payoff
- Top management frequently meets with employees, customers, suppliers on quality issues
- Managers' evaluation systems recognize quality as major priority; management behavior at all levels reflects this
- Managers engaged in removing barriers to excellence

- Extent to which quality values have been adopted throughout organization evaluated on periodic basis

---

60–40%
- Most top executives, managers fully support quality efforts, communicate organization's quality vision, goals, values
- TQM is a significant priority for many groups within organization; belief in continuous improvement permeates these groups; effective strategies used to involve many managers, supervisors in quality
- Some resources (time, training, dollars) invested to improve quality
- Communication often two-way (but primarily one-way), clear, consistent; departments frequently cooperate to achieve quality objectives
- "Ownership" of quality effort exercised by most groups within organization
- Top management committed to long-term quality improvement; supports some quality improvement projects that have only long-term payoff
- Top management has contact with employees, customers, suppliers on quality issues
- Managers' evaluation systems include measurable quality improvement objectives
- Managers have begun to remove barriers to excellence
- Extent to which quality values have been adopted throughout organization evaluated occasionally

---

40–20%
- Many top executives, managers supportive of/interested in quality improvement; quality awareness present in most areas
- Many groups convinced that TQM is important
- Some resources allocated to initiate quality improvement in a few areas
- Communication usually top-down (sometimes two-way); managers, supervisors encouraged to cooperate across departments
- Quality improvement projects underway; most aimed at specific short-term objectives/payoff
- Managers, supervisors encouraged to improve qual-

ity; plans in place to incorporate quality objectives into evaluation systems
- Management planning to remove some barriers to excellence
- Top management attuned to extent to which quality values have been adopted throughout organization

---

20–0%
- Top executives beginning to support quality-related activities; support tentative rather than whole-hearted, active
- A few key managers support quality improvement; quality awareness present among some work units
- Few resources allocated to quality improvement
- Communication primarily top/down; cooperation across departments occurs when problems or crises arise
- A few quality improvement projects underway in some areas; plans in place to begin others

2. STRATEGIC PLANNING (15 POINTS)

100–80%
- Short, long-term goals for quality improvement established across organization as part of overall strategic planning, budgeting process; goals require organization to "stretch"
- Operational plans at sub-organizational levels provide clear details for strategic plans; managers held accountable for attaining objectives
- Formal process established throughout organization to develop quality improvement goals, update plans periodically
- Principal types of quality data, information, analyses (customer requirements, process capabilities, supplier data, benchmark data) used in planning throughout organization
- Customer needs/expectations, issues relating to improved supplier relationships incorporated into quality improvement planning
- Benchmark data from best organizations in field used extensively for broad range of products, services, processes to determine potential quality improvements; strives to better benchmark organizations

- Employees participate in development of strategic/operational plans
- Key requirements such as technology, employee training, supplier quality formally assessed and compared to current status in those areas; needs factored into plans
- Planning process formally evaluated on regular basis; corrective actions taken to improve process

---

80–60%
- Short, long-term goals for quality improvement established across most of organization, included in overall budget planning
- Operational plans developed at most sub-organizational levels to link with strategic plan; managers held accountable for attaining major objectives
- Formal process established in most parts of organization to develop improvement goals, update plans periodically
- Principal types of quality data, information, analyses (customer requirements, process capabilities, supplier data, benchmark data) used in planning in most parts of organization
- Customer needs/expectations, issues relating to improved supplier relationships are significant factors in quality improvement planning process
- Benchmark data from similar organizations used for key products, services, processes to determine potential quality improvements; strives to match benchmark organizations
- Some employees participate in development of strategic/business plans
- Key requirements such as technology, employee training, supplier quality considered during planning process; some needs factored into plans
- Planning process evaluated on periodic/as-needed basis; some corrective actions taken
- Plans identify improvement priorities critical to organization's mission that will be relatively difficult to attain; resources allocated to support these objectives

---

60–40%
- Short, long-term goals for quality improvement established in key parts of organization
- Operational plans developed at key sub-organiza-

tional levels; managers held accountable for attaining major objectives

- Formal process established in key parts of organization to develop improvement goals, update plans periodically
- Some types of quality data, information, analyses (customer requirements, process capabilities, benchmark data) used in planning in key parts of organization
- Customer needs/expectations influence quality improvement planning process; some attention given to improved supplier relationships
- Benchmark data most readily available for major products, services; data used to determine potential quality improvements
- Some employees participate in development of operational plans
- Some procedure for evaluating planning process exists
- Plans identify improvement priorities central to organization's mission; plans aim for higher objectives each year; resources related to major goals

---

40–20%
- Goals for quality improvement established in parts of organization; managers develop objectives, details related to goals
- Improvement goals generally specified by management
- Customer needs generally known for key products/ services, considered in quality improvement planning process
- Only most general concerns given to key requirements during planning process
- Goals identify quality priorities that may not be central to organization's mission; goals do not require major effort or change in organization

---

20–0%
- General goals contain elements of quality improvement; quality planning not yet integrated with overall strategic planning
- Customer needs may not be routinely considered during planning process

- Implementation strategy for introducing TQM in organization is underway

3. FOCUS ON THE CUSTOMER (40 POINTS)

100–80%	• A variety of effective/innovative methods used to obtain customer (internal, external) feedback for all functions • Product/service features clearly specified in all customer feedback systems; features ranked in terms of relative importance • Effective well-defined systems in place linking customer feedback, complaints to groups that can act on information • Processes requiring improvement based on customer feedback receive priority attention; corrective action plans developed, implemented • Easy access by customers to information; problem resolution ensured • Management actively seeks ways to ensure that all employees are aware of customers' needs/expectations, understand, fulfill customer service standards • Customer-contact employees fully empowered to resolve customer problems • Recruiting practices identify people with specific personality traits conducive to harmonious customer-contact relations; training designed for customer-contact employees to elicit desired attitudes, behaviors • Service goals aimed at exceeding customer expectations; progress toward goals tracked, reported to relevant units, used for planning improvements • Feedback systems evaluated, improved to reflect changing customer concerns, complaints; validity/objectivity of monitoring methods ensured
80–60%	• Effective feedback systems used for all customers (external, internal) of major functions • Product/service features clearly specified in most feedback systems; features ranked in terms of relative importance

- Systems in place that link customer feedback to groups that can act on information
- Customer feedback acted on at appropriate levels; data used to take corrective action, improve processes
- Several improvements made in easing customer access to information, problem resolution
- Management ensures that all employees are aware of customers' needs/expectations, understand customer service standards
- Customer-contact employees empowered to resolve routine customer problems
- Specific training for customer-contact employees
- Service goals based on expectations of major internal customers, all external customers; progress toward goals tracked, used for planning
- Feedback systems in key areas evaluated, improved to reflect changing customer concerns, complaints; validity/objectivity ensured

---

60–40%
- Systems in place to solicit customer feedback on regular basis
- Product/service features clearly specified in most feedback systems
- Data from customer feedback systems sent to individual managers to plan, carry out corrective action
- Some improvements made in easing customer access to information, problem resolution; more improvements in planning stage
- Most work units aware of customers' needs/expectations, understand customer service standards
- Customer-contact employees identify customer problems for resolution at higher levels
- Some training for customer-contact employees
- Service goals, based on customer feedback, set for each major service to external customers
- Feedback systems in some areas evaluated, improved to reflect changing customer concerns, complaints

---

40–20%
- Most external, some internal customers identified; needs/expectations determined through ad hoc processes rather than systematic methods

- Customer feedback systems report on general satisfacation/dissatisfaction issues
- Customer feedback used in many areas to take corrective action
- Plans developed for easing customer access to information, problem resolution
- Customer service standards under development
- Some service goals set in key areas

20–0%
- Customer complaints major method for obtaining customer feedback
- Complaints handled on case-by-case basis, answered individually; may not be used systematically to improve processes
- Many work units have identified customers, begun to determine needs/expectations
- Some work units initiating methods for determining customer requirements, feedback
- Complaints concerning purchased goods/services may not be collected, used systematically
- Service goals focus on reducing complaints

---

4. EMPLOYEE TRAINING & RECOGNITION (15 POINTS)

100–80%
- Organization is implementing systematic, documented training plan, based on comprehensive needs analysis; effectiveness of quality education/training evaluated, improved on continuing basis
- Training plans fully integrated into overall strategic, quality planning; key strategies exist for increasing effectiveness, productivity of all employee groups
- Everyone trained in support of continuous improvement; focus of training on prevention of problems; technical skills continuously upgraded
- Frequent updates on new developments in quality improvement shared with entire organization
- Training investment shows clear evidence of human resource development priority
- Formal process exists to evaluate, recognize employee contributions
- Managers personally, regularly, fairly recognize individuals, teams for measurable contributions

- Rewards, recognition broad-based, innovative; encompass all levels of organization
- Increased emphasis on recognition of teamwork; balance achieved between individual, team recognition; celebration of small successes common
- Peer recognition important part of reward structure
- Favorable data regarding percent of employees, teams recognized in different employee categories, by type of recognition

---

80–60%
- Organization is implementing written training plan for deciding what quality education/training is needed; effectiveness of quality education/training periodically evaluated
- Training plans considered in overall strategic, quality planning process
- Nearly everyone trained in support of continuous improvement; focus on prevention of problems; technical skills upgraded based on data from quality measurement system
- Management meetings (Quality Councils) reinforce improvement methods, introduce new ideas
- New training developed to improve customer satisfaction; implementation on schedule
- Continued commitment of significant resources to training
- Process in place to recognize employee contributions; increased emphasis on recognition of teamwork
- Managers at most levels personally, regularly, fairly recognize individuals, teams for measurable contributions
- Celebration of small successes common in most parts of organization
- Peer recognition often used
- Positive trends over past two-five years in employee recognition

---

60–40%
- Organization's training plan being implemented on schedule; coordinated with quality improvement effort
- Most of organization trained in quality awareness, group problem solving to support continuous im-

provement; training emphasizes prevention of problems; technical skills upgraded periodically
- Most managers use quality improvement techniques, team development strategies
- Significant increase in training resource commitment over past practice
- Individuals, teams recognized for achievements; celebration of small successes common in many parts of organization
- Managers in majority of work units regularly, fairly recognize individuals, teams for measurable contributions
- Number of rewards for quality improvement increasing

40–20%
- Training plan under development
- Many parts of organization trained in group problem solving to support continuous improvement; ongoing training in technical skills offered
- Most managers have attended quality awareness sessions, learned quality improvement methods
- Resource commitment to training increased over past year
- Rewards, recognition heavily focused on individual efforts; some teams also recognized, rewarded
- Rewards, recognition for quality improvement employed in many parts of organization
- Number of rewards increased slightly over past year

20–0%
- Organization has plans to increase quality training; may not be specific
- Some parts of organization trained in quality awareness, group problem solving to support continuous improvement; training also offered in upgrading technical skills
- Many managers have attended quality awareness sessions; some have also learned quality improvement methods, group dynamics
- Minimal resources committed to quality training
- Rewards, recognition primarily for individual effort; some changes planned for recognizing teamwork
- Rewards, recognition may not be focused on quality improvement

- Number of rewards relatively constant from year to year

5. EMPLOYEE EMPOWERMENT & TEAMWORK (15 POINTS)

100–80%	• Innovative, effective employee involvement approaches used; several avenues available for participation in improvement efforts • Management provides environment that supports employee involvement, contribution, teamwork; positive atmosphere of trust/respect exists between management, employees • Cross-functional team cooperation occurs across organization to better meet customer needs; suppliers, customers routinely participate in team activity • Positive suggestion trends, acceptance rates, percent of employees making suggestions, team participation trends; other indicators of participation from all employees; quality of work life improving throughout organization • Employees have strong feeling of empowerment, team ownership of work processes; effective approaches exist to enhance employee authority to act • Employees feel "ownership" of quality improvement, exhibit personal pride in quality of work • Power, rewards, information, knowledge moved to lowest feasible levels; organization flattened substantially as result of employee empowerment • Improvement resulting from employee participation clearly evident in systems, processes, products/services • Formal survey process used on regular basis to determine levels of employee satisfaction; follow-up actions taken to improve organizational environment, human resource practices • Future plans address how to sustain momentum, enthusiasm • Union, management cooperate to achieve quality improvement
80–60%	• Many natural work groups constitute quality improvement teams; some innovative involvement

methods used; multiple avenues available for participation in improvement efforts

- Top management, majority of mid-managers support employee involvement, contribution, teamwork; trust/respect between management, employees typical of most of organization
- Cross-functional teams work on inter-unit, system-wide improvements; suppliers, customers participate in team activities that directly affect them
- Number of suggestions, rate of acceptance across organization growing; voluntary teams address work environment issues
- Steady increase in number of teams; high percentage of volunteers
- Most employees have strong feeling of empowerment, team ownership of work processes; authority to act enhanced for most employees
- Most employees feel "ownership" of quality improvement, exhibit personal pride in quality of work
- Power, rewards, information, knowledge moved to lower levels in organization; organization flattened as result of employee empowerment
- Substantial evidence that teams contribute to quality improvement
- Periodic survey process used to assess employee satisfaction; many changes desired by employees are made
- Future plans specifically include involvement of all employees; implementation on schedule
- Union, management have begun to work together on quality improvement issues

---

60–40%
- Majority of managers support employee involvement, contribution, teamwork; trust/respect between management, employees growing
- Variety of employee team activities; some cross-functional teams; some include participation of customers
- Percentage of employees involved in team activities, number of teams increased over past two years; number of suggestions increased over past two years
- Many employees feel "ownership" of quality improvement, exhibit personal pride in quality of work

- Some employees have feeling of empowerment, team "ownership" of work processes; authority to act enhanced for some employees
- Power, rewards, information, knowledge shared more widely, at lower levels than previously
- Evidence of improvements resulting from employee participation
- Informal surveys of employee satisfaction in major areas; some improvements made
- Plans to expand employee involvement gradually; implementation on schedule
- Union, management have initiated discussions on quality improvement issues

---

40–20%
- Many managers support employee involvement, contribution, teamwork; in these work units trust/ respect between management, employees growing
- Some quality improvement/problem-solving teams established; a few achieving improvements in work processes, products/services
- "Ownership" of quality improvement growing in work units that support employee involvement
- Number of employees on teams increased over past year
- Effective suggestion system; suggestions/ideas from employees increased over past year
- Employees queried regarding satisfaction; improvements may result
- Specific plans in place to increase employee team participation in several areas

---

20–0%
- Some managers support employee involvement, contribution, teamwork; most managers operate in more controlling mode
- Small percentage of employees participating in team activities; a few teams established
- Traditional suggestion system; number of suggestions relatively stable over past two-three years
- Improvements to organizational environment and human resource practices result from employee suggestions, complaints

- Only general, non-specific plans to expand employee involvement

6. MEASUREMENT & ANALYSIS (15 POINTS)

100–80%
- Quality, timeliness information collected on all products/services for external customers and from suppliers, and for all *significant* products/services for internal customers
- Comprehensive quality, timeliness, efficiency, effectiveness data available, measuring all aspects of organization's processes, products/services; measures available to all appropriate users
- Information collected is complete, timely, accurate, useful; benchmark data used for comparative purposes
- Routine, periodic checks made to ensure validity of data
- Employees across organization routinely use measures to identify problems, quantitative methodologies to identify solutions; assessment techniques verify that remedies produce expected results
- Appropriate, advanced technology/tools used in all work processes, information collection

---

80–60%
- Quality, timeliness information collected from most internal/external customers, suppliers
- Quality, timeliness, efficiency, effectiveness data available on most aspects of organization's processes, products/services; measures made available to all appropriate users
- Most information collected is complete, timely, accurate, useful; beginning to collect, use benchmark data
- Checks made to ensure validity of quality data
- Most work units use quality measures to identify problems and quantitative methodologies to identify solutions; assessment techniques verify that remedies produce expected results
- Appropriate, advanced technology/tools used in most work processes, information collection

60–40%	• Quality, timeliness information collected from major customers, suppliers, many internal operations
	• Quality, timeliness, efficiency, effectiveness data available on several aspects of organization's processes, products/services; measures made available to senior managers, other key personnel
	• Many work units use quality measures to identify problems, quantitative methodologies to identify solutions, techniques to verify that remedies produce expected results
	• Information collected usually complete, timely, accurate, useful
	• Appropriate, advanced technology/tools used in many work processes, information collection activities
40–20%	• Quality, timeliness information collected from some customers, internal operations
	• Limited data on quality, timeliness, efficiency, effectiveness available on organization's processes, products/services; some measures provided to narrow range of senior managers
	• Some work units use quality measures to identify problems and quantitative methodologies to identify solutions
	• Information may not be complete, timely; sometimes may not be accurate, useful
	• Appropriate, advanced technology/tools used in some work processes, information collection activities
20–0%	• Feedback system providing information on quality, timeliness in planning stages
	• Quality, timeliness, efficiency, effectiveness data not generally available; data primarily used for reporting purposes rather than improvement
	• A few work units beginning to use quality measures to identify problems, quantitative problem solving to identify solutions
	• Quality information presently collected on ad hoc basis
	• Outmoded technology/tools used in many work processes, information collection activities

7. QUALITY ASSURANCE (30 POINTS)

100–80%	• All products/services, processes designed, reviewed, verified, controlled to meet customer needs/expectations • Methods of process optimization, such as Taguchi's design of experiments, used routinely • Methods used to assure quality emphasize prevention, not detection • Comprehensive assessments of quality assurance systems performed at appropriate intervals; findings translated into improvements of systems • Quality assurance systems updated to keep pace with changes in technology, practice, quality improvement • Established methods used to verify quality requirements met by all suppliers; quality is key criterion used in selecting suppliers • Product/service-related standards set for all internal support functions
80–60%	• Majority of products/services, processes designed, reviewed, verified, controlled to meet customer needs/expectations • Methods of process optimization, such as Taguchi's design of experiments, generally used • Methods used to assure quality of most products/services emphasize prevention, not detection • Assessments of quality assurance systems performed at appropriate intervals • Quality assurance systems in most parts of organization updated to keep pace with changes in technology, practice, quality improvement • Established methods used in most parts of organization to verify that quality requirements met by all suppliers; quality is a criterion used in selecting suppliers • Product/service-related standards set for most internal support functions
60–40%	• Key products/services, processes designed, reviewed, verified, controlled to meet customer needs/expectations

- Methods of process optimization, such as Taguchi's design of experiments, occasionally used
- Methods used to assure quality of key products/services emphasize prevention, not detection
- Assessments conducted of quality assurance systems for key products/services performed at appropriate intervals
- Key areas use established method to verify quality requirements met by largest suppliers
- Product/service–related standards set for some internal support functions

---

40–20%
- A few products/services intended for outside customers designed, reviewed, controlled to meet customer needs/expectations
- Methods used to assure quality for most products/services emphasize detection, not prevention
- Some verification checks made to ensure quality requirements met by largest suppliers; may not be systematic, consistently performed

---

20–0%
- Products/services for customers reviewed, controlled to meet internally developed specifications; specifications may or may not include customer input
- Meeting quality requirements may not be priority for suppliers
- Systematic approach to quality assurance in planning stages; inspection remains primary tool of quality control

---

8. QUALITY & PRODUCTIVITY IMPROVEMENT RESULTS (50 POINTS)

100–80%
- Most significant indicators of performance demonstrate exceptional results; superior to competition in all areas; customer satisfaction shows improvement in each year over past five years
- Excellent results achieved in all dimensions (quality, timeliness, efficiency, effectiveness) across all areas
- Results clearly, strongly related to TQM approach
- Results sustained at high levels over past five years
- Results contribute significantly to organization's mission

- Quality performance of all suppliers uniformly improving over past five years

---

80–60%
- Most significant indicators of performance demonstrate excellent results; competitive in all areas; customer satisfaction trend is up over past five years
- Good results achieved in almost all dimensions (quality, timeliness, efficiency, effectiveness) across almost all areas
- Results related to TQM approach
- Results improving over past three years
- Results contribute to organization's mission
- Quality performance of most suppliers improving over past three years

---

60–40
- Most significant indicators of performance demonstrate good results; competitive in many areas, including customer satisfaction with quality of products/services
- Improvements achieved in several dimensions (quality, timeliness, efficiency, effectiveness) across many areas
- Results generally improving over past two years
- Results related to organization's mission
- Quality performance of some major suppliers improving over past two years

---

40–20%
- Most significant indicators of performance demonstrate improving results in several areas; including customer satisfaction
- Improvements achieved in one or more dimensions (quality, timeliness, efficiency, effectiveness) across several areas
- Quality of suppliers generally improving

20–0%
- Some results in one or more areas
- Results achieved in one or more dimensions (quality, timeliness, efficiency, effectiveness) in one or more areas
- Little evidence of improvement trends

Notes

Much of the material in this book was gathered from interviews and material collected while researching *Fortune*'s annual section on quality improvement between 1986 and 1991. We also omit detailed citations from standard statistical sources, such as federal agencies, and from recent events covered extensively in the business press. Full citations for published materials are given in the bibliography; short forms appear here.

Overview

1. White, "The Danger from Japan," 22.

1.

1. Dertouzos et al., *Made in America,* 9.
2. Garvin, *Managing Quality,* 22.
3. Ibid., 69.

2.

1. "Quality Illustrated."

3.

1. Womack et al., *The Machine That Changed the World,* 56.
2. Feigenbaum, "Engineering Quality as a World Marketing Strategy," 14.

3. Imai, *Kaizen,* 50.
4. Ohno, *Just-in-Time for Today and Tomorrow,* 23.
5. Shingo, *A Study of the Toyota Production System,* 106–107.
6. Yasuda, *40 Years, 20 Million Ideas,* 70–71.
7. Hay, *The Just-in-Time Breakthrough,* vii.
8. Livingston et al., *Postwar Japan,* 403.
9. Walton, *The Deming Management Method,* 247.
10. Wood, "A Lesson Learned and a Lesson Forgotten," 70.
11. Garvin, *Managing Quality,* 186.
12. Wood, 71.
13. Ishikawa, *What Is Total Quality Control,* 44.
14. Ibid., 45.
15. Ibid., 198.
16. Garvin, *Managing Quality,* 184.
17. Walton, *Deming Management Method,* 18–19.

4.

1. Young, speech.
2. Shook, *Turnaround,* 149.
3. Doody and Bingaman, *Reinventing the Wheels,* 45.
4. Ibid., 67.
5. Donis, speech.
6. Akao, *Quality Function Deployment,* preface.

5.

1. Pirsig, *Zen and the Art of Motorcycle Maintenance,* 255.
2. Drucker, *Innovation and Entrepreneurship,* 228.
3. Camp, *Benchmarking,* 72.

6.

1. "Productivity and Employment," 13.
2. Ibid., 23.
3. De Pree, *Leadership Is an Art,* 24.
4. Beer et al., "Why Change Programs Don't Produce Change," 159.
5. Ryan and Oestreich, *Driving Fear Out of the Workplace.*
6. Orsburn et al., *Self-Directed Work Teams,* 8–9.
7. Smith, F. W., "Creating an Empowering Environment for All Employees," 7.

8. "Roger Milliken Outlines Baldrige-Winning Philosophy," 1, 6.
9. "A Survey of Employees' Attitudes Toward Their Jobs and Quality."
10. Fisher, speech.
11. Prokesch, "Employees Go to the Rescue," D1, D3.
12. Pulos, *The American Design Adventure,* 78.
13. Ibid.

7.

1. Thurow, "A Time to Dismantle the World Economy," 22.

8.

1. Fallows, *More Like Us,* 48.
2. "Picking Up the Pace," 1.
3. "A Survey of Employees' Attitudes Toward Their Jobs and Quality."
4. Ibid.

9.

1. Carlzon, *Moments of Truth,* 83.
2. Artzt, "Winning the Global Market," 4.
3. Artzt, Analysts Meeting Speech, 8–10.
4. Parker and Slaughter, "Behind the Scenes at NUMMI Motors," 2.
5. Lee, "Worker Harmony Makes NUMMI Work," 2.
6. Sherman, "The Mind of Jack Welch."

Afterword

1. Thurow, "The State of American Competitiveness and How It Can Be Improved," 13.

Bibliography

Abegglen, James C., and George Stalk, Jr. *Kaisha, the Japanese Corporation.* New York: Basic Books, 1985.

Akao, Yoji. *Quality Function Deployment: Integrating Customer Requirements into Product Design.* Cambridge, Massachusetts and Norwalk, Connecticut: Productivity Press, 1990. Translated by Glenn H. Mazur and Japan Business Consultants Ltd. Originally published as *Hinshitukenai katuyou no jissai,* copyright © 1988 by Japan Standards Association.

Albrecht, Karl. *Service Within: Solving the Middle Management Leadership Crisis.* Homewood, Illinois: Dow Jones–Irwin, 1990.

———, and Ron Zemke. *Service America: Doing Business in the New Economy.* New York: Warner Books, 1990.

Artzt, Edwin L. Speech for the Analysts Meeting, Moscow, May 21, 1990.

———. "Winning the Global Market: Challenging Traditional Strategic Thinking." Speech for students at UCLA, Los Angeles, October 12, 1990.

Asaka, Tetsuichi, and Kazuo Ozeki (eds.). *Handbook of Quality Tools: The Japanese Approach.* Cambridge, Massachusetts and Norwalk, Connecticut: Productivity Press, 1990. Originally published as *Genbacho no tameno QC Hikkei,* copyright © 1988 by Japan Standards Association, Tokyo. English translation copyright © 1990 by Productivity Press.

Asman, David (ed.). *The Wall Street Journal on Managing: Adding Value Through Synergy.* New York: Doubleday/Currency, 1990.

Baida, Peter. *Poor Richard's Legacy: American Business Values From*

Benjamin Franklin to Donald Trump. New York: William Morrow, 1990.

Barry, Gerald J. "Stay Tuned." *The Quality Review,* Spring 1988, 34–39.

Beer, Michael, Russell A. Eisenstat, and Bert Spector. "Why Change Programs Don't Produce Change." *Harvard Business Review,* November–December 1990, 158–166.

Bell, Daniel. *The Cultural Contradictions of Capitalism.* New York: Basic Books, 1978.

Bennett, Amanda. *The Death of the Organization Man.* New York: William Morrow, 1990.

Bennis, Warren. *On Becoming a Leader.* Reading, Massachusetts: Addison-Wesley, 1989.

Berry, Leonard L., Valarie A. Zeithaml, and A. Parasuraman. "Quality Counts in Services, Too." *Business Horizons,* May–June 1985, 44–52.

Blackburn, Joseph D. (ed.) *Time-Based Competition: The Next Battleground in American Manufacturing.* Homewood, Illinois: Business One Irwin, 1991.

Bond, Helen. "Innovative Management." *Dallas Business Journal,* July 2, 1990.

Bowles, Jerry G. "Beyond Customer Satisfaction Through Quality Improvement." Fourth Annual Quality Improvement Section, *Fortune,* September 26, 1988.

———. "The Human Side of Quality." Sixth Annual Quality Improvement Section, *Fortune,* September 24, 1990.

———. "Quality: The Competitive Advantage." Third Annual Quality Improvement Section, *Fortune,* September 28, 1987.

———. "The Quality Imperative." Second Annual Quality Improvement Section, *Fortune,* September 29, 1986.

———. "The Race to Quality Improvement." Fifth Annual Quality Improvement Section, *Fortune,* September 25, 1989.

———. "The Renaissance of American Quality." First Annual Quality Improvement Section, *Fortune,* October 14, 1985.

Boyett, Joseph H., and Henry P. Conn. *Workplace 2000: The Revolution Reshaping American Business.* New York: Dutton, 1991.

Camp, Robert C. *Benchmarking: The Search for Industry Best Practices That Lead to Superior Performance.* Milwaukee: ASQC Quality Press, and White Plains, New York: Quality Resources, 1989.

Carlzon, Jan. *Moments of Truth.* New York: Harper & Row, Perennial Library edition, 1989.

"A CEO's Odyssey Toward World Class Manufacturing." *Chief Executive,* September 1990, 46–49.

Clausing, Don, and Bruce H. Simpson. "Quality By Design." *Quality Progress,* January 1990, 41–44.

Clifford, Donald K., Jr., and Richard E. Cavanagh. *The Winning Performance: How America's High-Growth Midsize Companies Succeed.* New York: Bantam Books, 1988.

Cohen, Stephen S., and John Zysman. *Manufacturing Matters: The Myth of the Post-Industrial Economy.* New York: Basic Books, 1987.

"Communicating Quality: 101 Companies Talk About How to 'Do It Right the First Time.'" Business Marketing, the Starmark Report III. Booklet published by Starmark, Inc., and Crain Communications, 1990.

Cound, Dana M. "Quality First." *Quality Progress,* March 1986.

Crocker, Olga L., Cyril Charney, and Johnny Sik Leung Chiu. *Quality Circles: A Guide to Participation and Productivity.* New York and Scarborough, Ontario: New American Library, Mentor Book edition, 1986.

Crosby, Philip B. *Let's Talk Quality: 96 Questions You Always Wanted to Ask Phil Crosby.* New York: McGraw-Hill, 1989.

"Customer Focus Research." Executive Briefing. Published by The Forum Corporation, April 1988.

"Dan River: Celebrating a Century of Progress 1882–1982." Company brochure, 1982.

De Pree, Max. *Leadership Is an Art.* New York: Dell Publishing, trade paperback, 1989.

Delta Consulting Group Inc. *The Emerging Architecture of Organizations: Structures and Processes for the 1990's.* New York: Delta Consulting Group, 1990.

Deming, W. Edwards. "It Does Work." From section "Product Quality USA: Quality—A Management Gambit." *Quality,* August 1980, Q26–31.

Dertouzos, Michael L., Richard K. Lester, Robert M. Solow, and The MIT Commission on Industrial Productivity. *Made in America: Regaining the Productive Edge.* Cambridge, Massachusetts, and London: The MIT Press, 1989.

Diebold, John. *The Innovators: The Discoveries, Inventions, and Breakthroughs of Our Time.* New York: Truman Talley Books/E. P. Dutton, 1990.

Donis, Peter. "The Genesis of Annual Quality Improvement at Caterpillar." Speech, Juran Institute Conference, Chicago, 1988.

Doody, Alton F., and Ron Bingaman. *Reinventing the Wheels: Ford's Spectacular Comeback.* Cambridge, Massachusetts: Ballinger Publishing Company, 1988.

Dreyfuss, Joel. "Reinventing IBM." *Fortune,* August 14, 1989, 30–39.

Drucker, Peter F. *Concept of the Corporation.* Second revised edition. New York and Scarborough, Ontario: New American Library, Mentor Book edition, 1983.

————. *Innovation and Entrepreneurship: Practice and Principles.* New York: Harper & Row, 1985.

————. *Managing for Results: Economic Tasks and Risk-taking Decisions.* New York: Harper & Row, Perennial Library edition, 1986.

————. *Managing the Non-Profit Organization: Practices and Principles.* New York: HarperCollins Publishers, 1990.

————. *The New Realities: In Government and Politics/ In Economics and Business/ In Society and World View.* New York: Harper & Row, 1989.

Eccles, Robert G. "The Performance Measurement Manifesto." *Harvard Business Review,* January–February 1991, 131–137.

Ernst and Young Quality Improvement Consulting Group. *Total Quality: An Executive's Guide for the 1990s.* Homewood, Illinois: Dow Jones–Irwin, 1990.

Fallows, James. *More Like Us: Making America Great Again.* Boston: Houghton Mifflin Company, 1989.

Feigenbaum, Armand V. "Engineering Quality as a World Marketing Strategy." *Professional Engineer,* June 1982, 12–17.

————. "Total Quality Control." *Harvard Business Review,* November–December 1956, 93–101.

Fisher, George. Transcription of a speech given at Center for Quality Management, Boston, July 10, 1990.

"Florida Utility Becomes First Overseas Company to Win Japan's Deming Prize." American Productivity & Quality Center *Letter,* March 1990, 1,7.

Gabor, Andrea. "The Man Who Changed the World of Quality." *International Management,* March 1988, 42–46.

————. *The Man Who Discovered Quality: How W. Edwards Deming Brought the Quality Revolution to America—the Stories of Ford, Xerox, and GM.* New York: Times Books, 1990.

Gale, Bradley T. "Beyond Customer Satisfaction: Four Key Mistakes Companies Make." *The Quality Executive,* October 1989, 8.

————. "How Quality Drives Market Share." *The Quality Review,* Summer 1987, 18–23.

Gardner, John W. "The Nature of Leadership: Introductory Considerations." Leadership Papers /1. The first in a series of papers prepared for the Leadership Studies Program sponsored by Independent Sector, Washington, D.C., January 1986.

—————. "The Tasks of Leadership." Leadership Papers/2. The second in a series of papers prepared for the Leadership Studies Program sponsored by Independent Sector, Washington, D.C., March 1986.

—————. "The Heart of the Matter: Leader-Constituent Interaction." Leadership Papers/3. The third in a series of papers prepared for the Leadership Studies Program sponsored by Independent Sector, Washington, D.C., June 1986.

—————. "Leadership and Power." Leadership Papers/4. The fourth in a series of papers prepared for the Leadership Studies Program sponsored by Independent Sector, Washington, D.C., October 1986.

—————. "The Moral Aspect of Leadership." Leadership Papers/5. The fifth in a series of papers prepared for the Leadership Studies Program sponsored by Independent Sector, Washington, D.C., January 1987.

Garvin, David A. *Managing Quality: The Strategic and Competitive Edge.* New York: The Free Press, 1988.

Geneen, Harold, with Alvin Moscow. *Managing.* New York: Avon Books, 1985.

Glen, Peter. *It's Not My Department! How to Get the Service You Want, Exactly the Way You Want It!* New York: William Morrow, 1990.

Goodman, John, Arlene Malech, and Theodore Marra. " 'I Can't Get No Satisfaction.' " *The Quality Review,* Winter 1987, 11–14.

Graham-Moore, Brian, and Timothy L. Ross. *Gainsharing: Plans for Improving Performance.* Washington, D.C.: The Bureau of National Affairs, Inc., 1990.

Grönroos, Christian. *Service Management and Marketing: Managing the Moments of Truth in Service Competition.* Lexington, Massachusetts: Lexington Books, 1990.

Gunn, Thomas G. *Manufacturing for Competitive Advantage: Becoming a World Class Manufacturer.* Cambridge, Massachusetts: Ballinger Publishing Company, 1987.

Halberstam, David. *The Reckoning.* New York: Avon Books, 1987.

Hansel, John L. "The Cult of Technical Rationality." *AACJC* (American Association of Community and Junior Colleges) *Journal,* March 1985, 39–41.

"The Hare and the Tortoise Revisited: The Businessman's Guide to Continuous Quality Improvement." Brochure published by American Society for Quality Control, 1989.

Hay, Edward J. *The Just-in-Time Breakthrough: Implementing the New Manufacturing Basics*. New York: John Wiley & Sons, 1988.

Hayes, Glenn E. *Quality & Productivity: The New Challenge*. Wheaton, Illinois: Hitchcock Publishing Company, 1985.

Heskett, James L. *Managing In the Service Economy*. Boston: Harvard Business School Press, 1986.

———, W. Earl Sasser, Jr., and Christopher W. L. Hart. *Service Breakthroughs: Changing the Rules of the Game*. New York: The Free Press, 1990.

"Hewlett-Packard Examines Manufacturing Excellence Beyond Its Backyard." American Productivity & Quality Center *Letter,* July 1989, 1, 6–7.

Hofheinz, Roy, Jr., and Kent E. Calder. *The Eastasia Edge*. New York: Basic Books, 1982.

Holusha, John. "No Utopia, But to Workers It's a Job." *New York Times,* Business section, January 29, 1989, 1, 10.

Horton, Thomas R. *"What Works For Me": 16 CEOs Talk About Their Careers and Commitments*. New York: Random House Business Division, 1986.

"How to Build Quality." *The Economist,* September 23, 1989, 91–92.

Iacocca, Lee, with William Novak. *Iacocca: An Autobiography*. New York: Bantam Books, 1986.

Imai, Masaaki. *Kaizen: The Key to Japan's Competitive Success*. New York: McGraw-Hill, 1986.

———. *Never Take Yes for an Answer: An Inside Look at Japanese Business*. Tokyo, Japan: The Simul Press, 1975.

Ishikawa, Kaoru. *What Is Total Quality Control: The Japanese Way*. Translated by David J. Lu. Englewood Cliffs, New Jersey: Prentice-Hall, 1985. Originally printed in Japan as *TQC towa Nanika-Nipponteki Hinshitsu Kanri* by Kaoru Ishikawa. © Kaoru Ishikawa 1984, 1981 published by JUSE Press. English language edition arranged through Japan Foreign-Rights Centre.

"John F. Akers: Turning the Corner at IBM." *The Quality Executive,* August 1989, 6–7.

Juran, J. M. "Made in USA: A Break in the Clouds." Summary address presented by Dr. J. M. Juran at "The Quest for Excellence," an executive conference featuring the 1989 Baldrige Award winners. © 1990 Juran Institute. This conference, February 22–23, 1990, in Washington, D.C., was sponsored by the National Institute of Standards and Technology in conjunction with the American Society for Quality Control and the American Productivity and Quality Center.

Kaihatsu, Hidy. "The New Xerox Movement: TQC in Japan." Speech presented by Hidy Kaihatsu, Director, International Relations Fuji Xerox at the Second Annual Quality Conference, New York City, May 16–17, 1989.

Karabatsos, Nancy. "Absolutely, Positively Quality." *Quality Progress,* May 1990, 24–28.

Katz, Donald R. "Coming Home." *Business Month,* October 1988, 57–62.

Keene, Margaret Rahn. *The Training Investment: Banking on People for Superior Results.* Homewood, Illinois: Business One Irwin, 1991.

Keller, Maryann. *Rude Awakening: The Rise, Fall, and Struggle for Recovery of General Motors.* New York: William Morrow and Company, 1989.

Kobayashi, Iwao. *20 Keys to Workplace Improvement.* Cambridge, Massachusetts, and Norwalk, Connecticut: Productivity Press, 1990. Originally published as *Shokuba Kaizen 20 Komoku,* copyright © 1988 by Brain Dynamics. English translation copyright © 1990 by Productivity Press. Translated by Warren W. Smith.

Kume, Hitoshi. "The Quality Cultural Exchange." *Quality Progress,* October 1990, 33–35.

Labich, Kenneth. "American Takes On the World." *Fortune,* September 24, 1990, 38–44.

———. "Hot Company, Warm Culture." *Fortune,* February 27, 1989, 74–78.

Lader, James I. "Getting Emotional About Quality." *The Quality Review,* Summer 1988, 32–37.

Lamb, Robert Boyden. *Running American Business: Top CEOs Rethink Their Major Decisions.* New York, Basic Books, 1987.

Lee, Bruce. "Worker Harmony Makes Nummi Work." *New York Times,* Business section, December 25, 1988, 2.

Levin, Doron P. "G.M. Saturn Plant Makes Friends." *New York Times,* January 23, 1990, D1, D7.

Lillrank, Paul, and Noriaki Kano. *Continuous Improvement: Quality Control Circles in Japanese Industry.* Ann Arbor, Michigan: Center for Japanese Studies, The University of Michigan, 1989. Michigan Papers in Japanese Studies No. 19.

Livingston, Jon, Joe Moore, and Felicia Oldfather (eds.). *Postwar Japan: 1945 to the Present.* New York: Pantheon Books, 1973.

" 'Made in America,' An Eight-Industry Study by MIT, Sets Five Imperatives for a More Productive America." *The Quality Executive,* June 1989, 1–3.

Magaziner, Ira C., and Robert B. Reich. *Minding America's Business:*

The Decline and Rise of the American Economy. New York: Vintage Books, 1983.

Matejka, Ken. *Why This Horse Won't Drink: How to Win—and Keep—Employee Commitment*. New York: AMACOM, 1991.

Matsumoto, Michihiro. *The Unspoken Way: Haragei: Silence in Japanese Business and Society*. Tokyo and New York: Kodansha International, 1988. Originally published in Japanese under the title *HARAGEI,* by Kodansha Ltd., 1984.

Melman, Seymour. *Profits Without Production*. New York: Alfred A. Knopf, 1983.

Miller, Lawrence M. *American Spirit: Visions of a New Corporate Culture*. New York: Warner Books, 1985.

———. *Barbarians to Bureaucrats: Corporate Life Cycle Strategies: Lessons from the Rise and Fall of Civilizations*. New York: Clarkson N. Potter, 1989.

MIT Commission on Industrial Productivity. *Working Papers of the MIT Commission on Industrial Productivity, Volume 1*. Cambridge, Massachusetts, and London, England: The MIT Press, 1989.

———. *Working Papers of the MIT Commission on Industrial Productivity, Volume 2*. Cambridge, Massachusetts, and London, England: The MIT Press, 1989.

Moffatt, George T. "New Initiatives in Quality Assurance." AT&T Bell Laboratories *Record,* December 1983.

Morita, Akio, with Edwin M. Reingold and Mitsuko Shimomura. *Made in Japan: Akio Morita and SONY*. New York: E. P. Dutton, 1986.

Morris, Charles R. *The Coming Global Boom: How to Benefit Now from Tomorrow's Dynamic World Economy*. New York: Bantam Books, 1990.

Nachi-Fujikoshi Corporation and Japan Institute of Plant Maintenance (eds.). *Training for TPM: A Manufacturing Success Story*. Cambridge, Massachusetts, and Norwalk, Connecticut: Productivity Press, 1990. Originally published in Japanese as *Fujikoshi no TPM* by the Japan Institute of Plant Maintenance, Tokyo. Copyright © 1986. English translation copyright © 1990 Productivity Press.

Nakane, Chie. *Japanese Society*. New York: Penguin Books, 1970.

Nanus, Burt. *The Leader's Edge: The Seven Keys to Leadership in a Turbulent World*. Chicago and New York: Contemporary Books, 1989.

Neimark, Jill. "Shake It Up!" *Success,* July/August 1988, 48–49.

"A New Era for Auto Quality." *Business Week,* October 22, 1990, 84–96.

Oberle, Joseph. "Quality Gurus: The Men and Their Message." *Training,* January 1990, 47–52.

O'Boyle, Thomas F. "Last In, Right Out: Firms' Newfound Skill in Managing Inventory May Soften Downturn." *Wall Street Journal,* November 19, 1990, A1, A6.

Ohmae, Kenichi. *The Mind of the Strategist.* New York: Penguin Books, 1983.

Ohno, Taiichi, with Setsuo Mito. *Just-in-Time for Today and Tomorrow.* Cambridge, Massachusetts, and Norwalk, Connecticut: Productivity Press, 1988. Translated by Joseph P. Schmelzeis, Jr. Originally published as *Naze hitsuyō na mono wo hitsuyō na bun dake hitsuyō na toki ni teikyo shinainoka?—Toyota seisan hooshiki kara keiei shisutemu e,* copyright © 1986 Diamond Inc., Tokyo. English translation copyright © 1988 Productivity Press.

Orsburn, Jack D., Linda Moran, Ed Musselwhite, John H. Zenger, with Craig Perrin. *Self-Directed Work Teams: The New American Challenge.* Homewood, Illinois: Business One Irwin, 1990.

Ouchi, William G. *Theory Z: How American Business Can Meet the Japanese Challenge.* New York: Avon Books, 1982.

Parasuraman, A. "Customer-Oriented Corporate Cultures Are Crucial to Services Marketing Success." *The Journal of Services Marketing,* Summer 1987, 39–46.

———, Valarie A. Zeithaml, and Leonard L. Berry. "A Conceptual Model of Service Quality and Its Implications for Future Research." Report published by Marketing Science Institute, August 1984.

———. "Servqual: A Multiple-Item Scale for Measuring Customer Perceptions of Service Quality." Marketing Science Institute research program working paper, August 1986.

Parker, Mike, and Jane Slaughter. "Behind the Scenes at Nummi Motors." *New York Times,* Business section, December 4, 1988, 2.

Pascale, Richard Tanner. *Managing on the Edge: How the Smartest Companies Use Conflict to Stay Ahead.* New York: Simon and Schuster, 1990.

———, and Anthony G. Athos. *The Art of Japanese Management: Applications for American Executives.* New York: Simon and Schuster, 1981.

"Pathways: New Thoughts on the Road to Quality Improvement." Brochure published by American Society for Quality Control, 1989.

"Picking Up the Pace: The Commercial Challenge to American Innovation." Booklet published by the Council on Competitiveness, 1989.

Pirsig, Robert M. *Zen and the Art of Motorcycle Maintenance*. New York: Bantam Books, a Bantam New Age Book, 1981.

"Productivity & Employment: Challenges for the 1990s." International Productivity Symposium III, April 10–13, 1988, Washington, D.C. Published by the U.S. Department of Labor, Bureau of Labor-Management Relations and Cooperative Programs, 1989.

Prokesch, Steven. "Employees Go to the Rescue: Labor Policy Aids Miller Furniture." *New York Times,* August 14, 1986, D1, D6.

Pulos, Arthur J. *The American Design Adventure: 1940–1975*. Cambridge, Massachusetts, and London, England: The MIT Press, 1990.

"Quality Illustrated." Brochure published by American Society for Quality Control, 1985.

Rayner, Bruce C. P. "Market-Driven Quality: IBM's Six Sigma Crusade." Special Report, "Commitment to Quality," *Electronic Business,* October 15, 1990.

"Refashioning IBM: Don't Just Stand There, Listen to Something." *The Economist,* November 17, 1990, 21–24.

Rehder, Robert R., and Marta Medaris Smith. "Kaizen and the Art of Labor Relations." *Personnel Journal,* December 1986, 83–93.

Reich, Robert B. *Tales of a New America*. New York: Times Books, 1987.

"The Revenge of Big Yellow." *The Economist,* November 10, 1990, 77–78.

"Roger Milliken Outlines Baldrige-Winning Philosophy." American Productivity & Quality Center *Letter,* December 1990, 1, 6.

Ryan, Kathleen D., and Daniel K. Oestreich. *Driving Fear Out of the Workplace: How to Overcome the Invisible Barriers to Quality, Productivity, and Innovation*. San Francisco: Jossey-Bass, 1991.

Schonberger, Richard J. *Building a Chain of Customers: Linking Business Functions to Create the World Class Company*. New York: The Free Press, 1990.

Schwartz, Stephen B. "Quality: The Key to Success in the '90s—and Beyond." Speech for the American Society for Quality Control, Southern Connecticut Division, Trumbell, Connecticut, June 13, 1990.

Senge, Peter M. *The Fifth Discipline: The Art and Practice of the Learning Organization*. New York: Doubleday/Currency, 1990.

"Service Quality: Measuring Customer Expectations." Booklet published by Metropolitan Life and affiliated companies, 1988.

Sewell, Carl, and Paul B. Brown. *Customers for Life: How to Turn that One-Time Buyer into a Lifetime Customer*. New York: Doubleday/Currency, 1990.

Sheridan, John H. "World-Class Manufacturing." *Industry Week,* July 2, 1990.

Sherman, Stratford P. "The Mind of Jack Welch." *Fortune,* March 27, 1989.

Shingo, Shigeo. *A Study of the Toyota Production System from an Industrial Engineering Viewpoint.* Revised edition. Cambridge, Massachusetts, and Norwalk, Connecticut: Productivity Press, 1989. Newly translated by Andrew P. Dillon. Originally published as *Study of 'TOYOTA' Production System from Industrial Engineering Viewpoint,* copyright © 1981 by Shigeo Shingo. Original English language edition published by Japan Management Association, 3-1-22 Shiba Park, Minato-ku, Tokyo. Retranslated into English by Productivity, Inc. English retranslation copyright © 1989 by Productivity, Inc.

Shook, Robert L. *Turnaround: The New Ford Motor Company.* New York: Prentice Hall Press, 1990.

Sloan, Alfred P., Jr. *My Years With General Motors.* Edited by John McDonald with Catharine Stevens. With a new introduction by Peter F. Drucker. New York: Doubleday/Currency, 1990.

Smith, Douglas K., and Robert C. Alexander. *Fumbling the Future: How Xerox Invented, Then Ignored, the First Personal Computer.* New York: William Morrow, 1988.

Smith, Frederick W. "Creating an Empowering Environment for All Employees." *The Journal for Quality and Participation,* June 1990, 6–10.

———. "Our Human Side of Quality." *Quality Progress,* October 1990, 19–21.

Stratton, Brad. "A Beacon for the World." *Quality Progress,* May 1990, 60–65.

Sullivan, L. P. "The Seven Stages in Company-Wide Quality Control." *Quality Progress,* May 1986, 77–83.

"Surprise! CEOs Blame Workers for Poor Quality." *The Quality Executive,* August 1990, 3.

"A Survey of Employees' Attitudes Toward Their Jobs and Quality." Survey conducted by the Gallup Organization for the American Society for Quality Control. Milwaukee: ASQC, 1990.

Taylor, Alex, III. "The New Drive to Revive GM." *Fortune,* April 9, 1990, 52–61.

Taylor, Frederick Winslow. *The Principles of Scientific Management.* New York and London: W. W. Norton & Company, 1967.

Thurow, Lester. "The State of American Competitiveness and How It Can Be Improved." Report of proceedings from The Xerox

Quality Forum II, July 31–August 2, 1990, Leesburg, Virginia, 13–16.

———. "A Time to Dismantle the World Economy." *The Economist,* November 9, 1985, 21–26.

"Training America: Learning to Work for the 21st Century." Booklet published by the American Society for Training and Development, 1989.

Uttal, Bro. "Companies That Serve You Best." *Fortune,* December 7, 1987, 98–116.

Walton, Mary. *Deming Management at Work.* New York: G. P. Putnam's Sons, 1990.

———. *The Deming Management Method.* New York: Perigee Books, 1986.

Waterman, Robert H., Jr. *The Renewal Factor: How the Best Get and Keep the Competitive Edge.* New York: Bantam Books, 1988.

Weinstein, Martin E. "Our Debt to Henry Ford." *Business Tokyo,* April 1990, 42–45. Condensed and reprinted. Originally published in *The Human Face of Japan's Leadership,* Praeger Publishers, New York, 1989. Copyrighted © 1989 by Martin E. Weinstein.

Welch, John F., Jr. "Quality—The Marketing Mission." Speech presented to the 1980 General Electric Marketing Management Conference, The Homestead, Hot Springs, Virginia, April 10, 1980.

———. "Speed, Simplicity, Self-Confidence: Keys to Leading in the '90s." Speech presented at The General Electric Annual Meeting of Share Owners, Greenville, South Carolina, April 26, 1989.

White, Theodore H. "The Danger from Japan." *New York Times Magazine,* July 28, 1985.

Whitely, Richard C. *The Customer-Driven Company: Moving From Talk to Action.* Reading, Massachusetts: Addison-Wesley, 1991.

Wiggenhorn, William. "Motorola U: When Training Becomes an Education." *Harvard Business Review,* July–August 1990, 71–83.

Wood, Robert Chapman. "A Lesson Learned and a Lesson Forgotten." *Forbes,* February 6, 1989, 70–78.

———. "The Prophets of Quality." *The Quality Review,* Fall 1988, 20–27.

Womack, James P., Daniel T. Jones, and Daniel Roos. *The Machine That Changed the World.* New York: Rawson Associates and Toronto, Ontario: Collier Macmillan Canada, 1990.

"Workplace Basics: The Skills Employers Want." Booklet published by the American Society for Training and Development and the

U.S. Department of Labor, Employment and Training Administration, 1988.

Wyden, Peter. *The Unknown Iacocca*. New York: William Morrow, 1987.

Yamashita, Toshihiko. *The Panasonic Way: From a Chief Executive's Desk*. Translated by Frank Baldwin. Tokyo and New York: Kodansha International, 1989. First published in Japanese in 1987 by Toyo Keizai Shinposha under the title of *Boku demo shacho ga tsutomatta*.

Yasuda, Yuzo. *40 Years, 20 Million Ideas: The Toyota Suggestion System*. Cambridge, Massachusetts, and Norwalk, Connecticut: Productivity Press, 1991. Originally published as *Toyota no soi kufuteian katsudo,* copyright © 1989 by Japan Management Association, Tokyo. Translated into English by Productivity Press.

Young, John A. Speech, Matsushita Quality Conference, Tokyo, July 1988.

Zeithaml, Valarie A., A. Parasuraman, and Leonard L. Berry. *Delivering Quality Service: Balancing Customer Perceptions and Expectations*. New York: The Free Press, 1990.

Zemke, Ron, with Dick Schaaf. *The Service Edge: 101 Companies That Profit From Customer Care*. New York: A Plume Book, 1990.

Zuboff, Shoshana. *In the Age of the Smart Machine: The Future of Work and Power*. New York: Basic Books, 1988.

Index